DATE DUE

JUL - 8 2004			

F

DEMCO 38-296

WHITE MISCHIEF

A CULTURAL HISTORY OF COCAINE

TIM MADGE

THUNDER'S MOUTH PRESS

NEW YORK

FOR LAURA—FOR EVERYTHING

CONTENTS

ACKNOWLEDGEMENTS

LIKE ALL BOOKS, this one could only have been written with the help of a large number of people. In the case of this work most, understandably, wish to remain as anonymous helpers. They know who they are, and all have provided me with a valuable and, at times, quite astonishing insight into the subject on which I have written.

More conventionally, three libraries have been of immense value: the Wellcome Library, the Drugscope Library and the British Library. Each of these libraries' collections on coca and cocaine were uniquely useful. I would like to thank the staff at each, all of whom has been so helpful in enabling me to source material, often at very short notice. At my publishers I have been helped by the sterling efforts of my editor, Deborah Kilpatrick, to whom a very special mention, and by Tina Hudson. Thanks as well to Sheil Land and my agent, Luigi Bonomi.

There is one person to whom, as so often and in so many things, I owe a great debt: for her consistent helpfulness; her support whenever there were crises or difficulties; and in her direct assistance checking through the original manuscript: Laura Ivill, who at last gets the dedication she deserves in one of my books. Whether she is pleased with the final result, only she knows. Any mistakes or errors of commission or omission remain, as always, with the author.

FOREWORD

ALTHOUGH THIS IS PRIMARILY A CULTURAL HISTORY of cocaine and its uses, I begin with the known early history of the plant, the leaves of which cocaine is extracted from – the coca plant, *Erythroxylum coca*. The coca plant is not merely the natural source of a very powerful drug. Chewing the leaves to get a mild high has been, and still is, an integral part of the lives of millions of people in South America. No one knows how this practice began, but the plant was famously revered by the Inca, who believed it had sacred origins. On those grounds, its use was limited for many hundreds of years. To gain a full understanding of the history of cocaine, we have to delve into the long-existing traditions of the Andeans. We must try to grasp what it is about the coca plant and its effects that finally led to nineteenth-century European chemists isolating the alkaloid they chose to call cocaine.

Coca leaves are used – with the cocaine content removed – in the world's most popular soft drink, Coca-Cola (from whence the name derives). Coca-Cola drew its inspiration from Vin Mariani, a popular mix of coca leaf and French wine of which millions of bottles were sold throughout the last half of the nineteenth century at a time when many believed that the coca leaf was a food of the gods. Much of the 'research' done at that time on the coca leaf may now be dismissed as amateurish dabbling, mixed as it was with travellers' tales from the south as well as much mythological hyperbole surrounding the Inca. The culmination of this craze was an extraordinary book written by W. Golden Mortimer, *History of Coca*, which is an anthem to the glory of the coca leaf more than anything else.

Today, anyone who has tried coca tea, or chewed coca leaves – legally – in parts of South America will attest to the plant's powers, mild in one sense but definitely an effective pick-me-up. Much detailed research still needs to be done on the leaves, but evidence exists to suggest that the coca leaf is worthy of further study.

Cocaine, the heart of this story, has an altogether different history. Its impact on the past hundred or so years has been intermittent but startling. Cocaine has been understandably demonised more than once over the years. Its most recent manifestation – as a smokable drug – has caused more anguish and misinformation than most other drugs classed, as it is, among the most dangerous (or powerful, depending on your point of view) known to humankind. There are entire cultures associated with the use of cocaine, jet-setters and the poor of the ghetto being just two. These diverse cultures have emerged more in the past twenty years than in any other time since cocaine was first synthesised.

It is a drug that, from every point of view, seems set to be with us for a very long time. We need to understand more about cocaine, to contextualise it in history, to see the errors made in the past over handling it and the mistakes we are making now in terms of policy, supply and use. These mistakes come from all directions – from the authorities who would ostensibly rid the world of it, to the illegal jungle laboratories still expanding their supply and the millions of users who show no sign of reducing their own demand.

TIM MADGE, 2001

INTRODUCTION

IN THE BEGINNING . . .

COCA LEAF AND COCAINE: light and dark, good and evil, God and the Devil. It is too easy an opposition to set up, too facile an answer to the questions which surround the natural and the artificial, the plant and the chemical. There are some kernels of truth, however, in this juxtaposition of the ways in which these two substances have been, and continue to be, used by millions of people all over the world. This situation looks set to continue, for there is no sign that interest in and desire for coca and cocaine are waning. If anything, it continues to rise, fuelled by a potent mix of the effect this drug has on the individual, the thrill of the illicit, the endorsements of the rich and famous and the apparently insatiable desire of the human mind for new experiences.

A hundred years ago interest in both coca leaf and cocaine was at fever pitch in the United States; in Europe a more restrained, but nonetheless fairly open, view still prevailed. Both the leaf and the alkaloid derived from it were still legal, both heavily endorsed by numbers of doctors, sellers of cure-alls, burgeoning pharmaceutical companies and many well-known individuals from the sciences and the arts. The nascent but rapidly growing Coca-Cola Company in the USA was still using the pure coca leaf to add zest and flavour to its drink. In Europe, Vin Mariani, the 'role model' for Coca-Cola, was close to its apogee.

Everything changed in the decade after 1901; everything and, as it has turned out, nothing. Karl Marx wrote that those who do not learn from history are condemned to repeat it; the story of coca and cocaine amply demonstrates his point. But first we must go on a journey in time and space, to put some perspective into this jumbled tale. We have, too, to consider our own relationship to this issue, and beyond that, to the broader question of what I will be calling recreational and cultural drug use. Coca chewing (as with traditional uses of marijuana and opium in other cultures) is locked into an ancient set of South American values, tied to a way of life that still continues. Then we must return to the present day, to make some kind of comparison with both the far past and the near. Have we learned anything at all from the way in which we have treated this drug in particular, and other drugs and their uses in general?

Because so much of the 'drugs debate' in our modern life is beset with confusion and doubt, and often charged with a highly emotive moral tone, the reader ought to understand from the start where this author is coming from. First, I have at times in the past been a user of recreational drugs. I say 'user' rather than the more conventional term 'have tried', because in the hypocrisy surrounding drugs use, many people imply by the word 'tried' that it was only once and that, also axiomatically, they did not much like the experience. Neither is likely to be true. Although my private life remains important to myself, my family and friends, it is relevant that the reader knows I have tried cocaine on one or two occasions in the past.

I believe that we have tied ourselves into an impossible knot on this entire issue. Unless we undo what we have done, legislatively and culturally, the problems surrounding recreational drug use will continue to beset us. I would seek to find ways to license their use – not so that they had to be prescribed by medics, but so that a reasonable level of both self and official monitoring of individual use could be maintained. I believe that were alcohol to be re-invented as the recreational drug it is today, a similar system would be put in place. In some senses, of course, it already exists with the Licencing Laws. If the current crop of recreational drugs were made legal, at a single stroke a huge part of international criminal activity would be felled, a mass of prisoners could be released and government exchequers all over the world would begin to receive huge additional tax revenues. Those people who are addicted (as with alcohol, they exist in some numbers) would be treated, not excoriated and punished. The mass of petty crime which effectively is the result of current drug policies would be drastically reduced. Many otherwise non-criminal people would be moved to the right side of the law.

There is a world of difference between current cocaine use, even at moderate levels, and coca leaf-chewing. Coca is an integral part of the lives of millions of ordinary law-abiding people in South America, where the coca leaf is legally grown. As we shall see later in the book, the United States is now apparently set on eradicating the entire coca crop used for chewing, in the process wrecking or seriously distorting whole economies and a way of life that has existed since these regions were first settled.

Coca leaf is a mild stimulant, chewed daily as a matter of course by many in the Amazon region and the Andes. When coca leaves are masticated with a variety of chemicals – lime or calcium carbonate, for instance – they act as a mild high, giving the chewer a feeling of energy and mental clarity, and reducing hunger, thirst or tiredness. These effects are very similar to those produced by a cup of tea or coffee, or by a cigarette. Even when coca is chewed over several hours, the effects are very different from those of cocaine. One researcher has suggested that the difference is like that between travelling by donkey or by jet aeroplane.

The high Andes of South America, intensely cold with relatively little oxygen and harsh ultraviolet light, is a highly stressful environment in which to live, probably among the most exhausting that people have inhabited for any length of time. Even those who have spent their entire lives in these harsh conditions find it hard. In these circumstance, chewing coca helps. The leaves are heavily chewed in the *puna*, the high Andean grasslands, where a subsistence economy exists, largely based on potato-growing and sheep-herding. Lower down, coca is used less. It is still important, though, not least as a medium of social interaction and religious ritual. The Indians in these regions have chewed coca since before the Incas, and have adapted their myths and religion to incorporate the coca plant.

Coca is chewed in specific ways, rather than simply cramming the leaves into the mouth as western tourists have been observed to do. An invitation to chew coca is an invitation to take part in a social occasion. One researcher has observed that friends who meet on the road will sit down to chew; and men who work in the fields will settle down to chew it before beginning their labour. When something serious or troubling has happened, shared coca leaf-chewing helps to alleviate the problem and express the participants' commitment to a rational and peaceful resolution to whatever is ailing them. Adults will chew coca after each of their three daily meals, as well as stopping for a coca break mid-morning and mid-afternoon, just as Europeans and North Americans will have coffee and tea breaks. When people settle down and open their coca bundles, each will offer their companions small, carefully composed bundles of the leaves, saying something like 'Let's chew coca together'. There are many rituals attached to chewing, involving the status of the chewers as well as what is being talked about. In short, it is a subtle and complex practice, with as many undertones as a Japanese tea ceremony.

As with the tea ceremony, there are religious undertones. Once the coca bag is opened, an individual will blow on the bundle while waving it in front of his or her mouth, invoking the earth (*Pacha Mama*) or sacred places or the community. For Andeans every landmark is experienced as alive and powerful, possessing a name and a personality. The earth as a whole is thought to be alive and to be primarily female. This is by no means based on some cloying sentimentality about 'mother earth', but on a profound and meaningful connection with the natural world. Coca is the medium by which men and women talk to the earth and its powerful, unpredictable deities.

Coca, then, is a means of communication, a transmitter sending messages between people and their gods. In many respects it is possible to see a connection between coca in this context and the body of Christ, as symbolised by the bread in the Christian communion service. Indeed, Indians will refer to coca as '*Hostia*', the host, explicitly making the same point. Coca-chewing is a means of social intercourse – orderly relations – linked to the sacred. It is this embedded and harmless culture which is now under threat from Western governments led by the USA. Legal coca is becoming harder to find and the governments of Colombia, Peru and Bolivia in particular are under huge pressure to stop both legal production and legal use. This is a little like banning all cars because some people are bad drivers.

What, then, are these millions of people doing, and what happens when they chew coca leaves? The chewing method hardly varies throughout this vast area. The leaf is always dried before use. This helps the rapid release of the alkaloids, of which cocaine is just one of fourteen. It is worth noting here that hardly any of the other alkaloids have been studied in any depth. The dried leaves are placed in the mouth a few at a time and slowly moistened with saliva. Almost at once a green juice begins to flow from the leaves, making them soft and pliable. They are then moved about in the mouth, rolled with the tongue into a ball and pushed into a cheek. The coca is never really chewed; rather the quid of leaves is sucked to extract the juices which then trickle into the stomach. The addition of an alkali, like lime (calcium oxide) or powdered ashes, helps to counteract the bitterness. This alkali not only sweetens the quid but also makes the juice much more potent, causing the cocaine release to numb the cheeks and increase the degree of stimulation. The alkali is carried in a little gourd. Coca generally has a grassy or hay-like taste.

South American coca chewers have a number of words for what they do: in Colombia it is *mambear*; in Peru and Bolivia *chacchar*, *acullicar*, *pijchear*; in general, it is *coquear*, or *mascar*. The amount kept in the mouth varies (from 25–75 grammes), along with the time, usually from 30 to 90 minutes, after which the ball of coca is spat out. All coca leaves contain cocaine. By weight, it is usually less than 1 per cent; Amazonas coca has less than 0.5 per cent. An important part of the leaves contain nutrients, again a subject which has hardly been studied. These nutrients include vitamins and minerals. Coca has been found to be higher in calories, proteins, carbohydrates, fibres, calcium, phosphorus, iron, vitamin A and riboflavin than 50 other local foodstuffs. Coca does produce a temporary suppression of appetite, but it is generally chewed after eating, not consumed as a way of deliberately suppressing the appetite nor as a substitute for food, as has been held.

There is no evidence that coca-chewing results in tolerance or physiological dependence, or has any acute or chronic long-term effects. The principal use of coca is for work and social occasions, the former simply because chewing the leaves helps keep people going. It is chewed by farmers, herders, miners and even fishermen. It is especially valued for making long journeys on foot, but this may be a remnant of the past, when Inca messengers were specifically supplied with it for this purpose.

The coca leaf is also used as medicine, a practice bound up in its overall cultural significance. It is taken internally as well as being chewed and is mostly used for ailments related to the gastro-intestinal tract, dysentry, stomach-ache, indigestion, diarrhoea, stomach ulcers and cramps. It is, of course, best known in many North American and European quarters as a treatment for altitude sickness; as an extension from its relief of acute mountain sickness (AMS) symptoms, it is also used for hangovers, dizziness or severe headache.

In the Amazonian basin, various tribes make the leaves into powder and swallow it, using as much as a pound of the powder a day. As with chewing, swallowing the powder appears from research not to lead to addiction in any form other than, possibly, psychological. It is as powder that cocaine has come to be best known in the rest of the world. Although snorted (as well as smoked) heavily in parts of South America, our journey leads us naturally back to North America and Europe, where cocaine first made its public appearance, about 115 years ago. And, although it was first injected, a route which leads to an almost instantaneous high as well as a possible heavy psychological addiction, most people snort the powder.

Cocaine, however, does not start as powder. The process of turning coca leaves into cocaine is a complex one, involving three separate stages: leaf to crude cocaine; crude to rock; rock to flake. The first two stages are vital to the extraction of usable cocaine and the last helps refine the product. Turning coca leaf into crude is usually done close to the growing areas and vats holding up to 15 tonnes are used. A tonne of coca leaf will yield between 33–44kg of cocaine (a crude street value of between £3–5m, if you assume the average 'quality' cocaine is 50 per cent cut and the price about £50 per gramme).

In stage one, a vat is filled with powdered coca leaves. Dilute sulphuric acid is added to leach out the cocaine along with the other alkaloids. Next, sodium carbonate is added to make an alkaline solution and precipitate the cocaine and other alkaloids. A light petroleum fraction, like benzene, is now stirred in; the benzene 'takes up' the cocaine and the other alkaloids. The resulting solution is drawn off from the top and washed to remove any residual acid (in an alkaline solution cocaine is insoluble in water, so none is lost at this stage). The washed solution is once more treated with sulphuric acid and vigorously stirred for up to three-quarters of an hour to redissolve the cocaine. After standing, the cocaine sulphate, with the sulphates of the other alkaloids, is drawn off again, leaving the benzene for re-use. This acidic solution is again treated with sodium carbonate to precipitate the cocaine; it is left to stand for about 12 hours, after which it is filtered.

The precipitate of cocaine is then washed with distilled water to remove residual acids and pressed into paste, sometimes in round containers like large cake tins. Once in this form, it is refined further. First, the paste is dissolved in dilute hydrochloric acid. It is then treated with potassium permanganate, which destroys the other alkaloids before 'attacking' the cocaine. This action is checked by the addition once more of sodium carbonate, which precipitates the cocaine before the mixture is filtered. As it dries the mixture coheres, turning into 'rock' cocaine. It is in this form that most people are likely to come across it. Rock cocaine is about 70 per cent pure, although if care has been taken the purity can be as high as 85 per cent. Buying rock cocaine does not guarantee it has not been cut with other substances and re-caked, but being able to tell the purity of the street product is down to experience and trust in the buyer.

Rock cocaine can be refined further. It is first pulverised into a powder and then dissolved in an alkaline solution. Ether, to 'take up' the cocaine once more, is added, and then methanol or hydrochloric acid. This precipitates the cocaine and the liquid is filtered off. This process can provide up to 99 per cent pure cocaine which, of course, can be cut in any number of ways and with any number of substances. Cocaine crudely 'purified' with petrol, rather than ether, will smell of petrol.

Cocaine snorted is almost invariably cut with other substances, usually speed (amphetamines) or 'freeze', other forms of anaesthetic, or both. These substances will lend to the user the illusion of the known effects of cocaine, numbing and a high, but the pure stuff is much more subtle. It takes longer to come into effect, but shortly gives the user a tremendous feeling of well-being and almost superhuman strength, allied with a powerful belief in his or her prowess. It may provide a sexual charge but, as with alcohol which reduces inhibitions, cocaine may well not allow a man, at least, to perform well – that is, if usage is common. Used every now and then it is most certainly an aphrodisiac for men and women alike. There is a view, though, that the so-called aphrodisiac effects of cocaine have much more to do with the user's knowledge that he or she has just shoved something very expensive *and* illegal up their nose.

All pure cocaine has a distinctive smell and a bitter taste, not unpleasant. It is as cocaine hydrochloride that it is generally snorted and, because refining is often less than perfect, a residual amount of acid remains in the powder. It is this which leads to a deterioration of the mucous membranes in the nose and which, if cocaine is used heavily over a number of years, can lead to the collapse of the septum and even, in extreme cases, the entire bridge of the nose.

Crack cocaine, over which there remains a considerable cloud, is derived from putting cocaine hydrochloride with bicarbonate of soda in some form of pipe and smoking the two together. As the two chemicals combine, there is a cracking sound. Cocaine used in this way is usually crude and it comes cheap. The high from crack is considerable but fleeting, because the cocaine is poor, leaving the user with a craving – like having a chocolate bar snatched away after only a taste.

Well-off cocaine users may from time to time use 'freebase' cocaine, where the hydrochloride is turned into a base of the drug using either ether or ammonia. If the hydrochloride sells in the UK for about £50–60 a gramme at the time of writing (early 2001), the freebase sells for £70–80 a gramme. It can be smoked in a variety of ways. Some use an ash filter, sucking the smoke strongly into the lungs. To create this effect, a powerful flame is applied to a rock of the freebase held on the bed of ash, usually on a small hash pipe. The hot smoke is hard to hold in the lungs, but it does give a powerful rush, strong enough to buckle the legs. It might be thought that inhaling highly acidic hot smoke into the lungs is not such a good idea: it isn't. But if good cocaine hydrochloride is morish (and it is), freebase is far more so. To increase the hit many people using freebase will fill a plastic bottle with the smoke (thus cooling it a little) and then inhale, getting a huge rush.

That use of cocaine is becoming much more commonplace is evident in a number of ways. First from newspaper reports of the number of celebrities, media people, actors, VIPs of various kinds, who have confessed to having used it (it is almost invariably the case that they refer to use in the past, not the present and never the future). Second, the ways in which television and film knowingly refer to cocaine use, quite often in comedies. A fairly large number of the BBC TV series *Absolutely Fabulous*, dealing with the antics of a female fashion journalist and a female PR company owner, contained references to cocaine and even footage of snorting (one episode had journalist Patsy unwittingly snorting plaster of Paris). Third, personal knowledge of people who will admit to having used cocaine from time to time, if they can get hold of some. This author first came across it, but did not use any, at a wedding he attended. Weddings, hen and stag nights, parties in general, even occasionally dinner parties, may all involve someone producing cocaine. The willingness of an increasing number of people to ask 'has anyone got any charlie' (among the commonest slang words for cocaine in the UK) is another indicator, as is the relative ease with which it can be obtained, and at a high quality, too.

Finally, and intriguingly, there have been a number of people who, having personal knowledge of the writer and knowing this book was being researched, have expressed a desire to try it for the first time. These requests, I feel bound to insist, I have never acceded to, nor ever would or could.

All this points to one of the more interesting aspects of cocaine: crack cocaine notwithstanding, the drug's image is cleaner than that of almost all the others. One reason, as we shall see, is to do with its history and the ways in which it was endorsed – and by whom. Another, due to its cost, has been its association with the rich and famous: the epithet 'champagne drug' is highly appropriate. Then there is the question of whether or not cocaine is addictive. On the accepted basis that a truly addictive substance has to produce three elements in an addict: dependence, tolerance and withdrawal, the last does not apply to cocaine; there are question marks over the first two. It is likely, though, that there is a medium to long-term problem of pyschological dependence. This subtly addictive quality has also been laid at the door of the coca leaf. More significant are the testimonies of those known 'coke addicts' who often report that, although no longer users, they dream about cocaine frequently. In this respect, it may ressemble nicotine.

Perhaps before delving into the origins of what remains a twentieth and twenty-first-century conundrum, and one that includes all recreational drugs and our relationships with them, it is worth quoting from one source on the subject of cocaine. Julie Burchill, the British author and journalist, writing about a British soap-opera star (Daniella Westbrook) who had destroyed her nasal septum through massive overuse of cocaine (it is alleged that she used up to six grammes a day over many years), wrote the following in the *Guardian* of 6 June 2000:

> 'Between 1986 and 1996, I must have put enough toot up my admittedly sizeable snout to stun the entire Colombian armed forces, and still it sits there, Romanesque and proud, all too bloody solid actually, unmistakably my father's nose . . . But unlike my wussy compadres, who used to get teary and bleary as the sun came up, I never found cocaine a problem; as one who suffers chronically from both shyness and a low boredom threshold, I simply can't imagine that I could have had any kind of social life without it, let alone reigned queen of the Groucho Club for a good part of the '80s and '90s. I don't regret my years as a cokehead, and, in fact, look back on them with affection; a whole decade went by in a blur, like some crazy Aerosmith video. But, gee, it was laffs.'

Conventionally, at this stage there comes a counter argument: I confess I have none. Anecdotal evidence, as well as official research, suggests moderate cocaine use appears to be all right; it might well be 'a laugh'. Recent surveys have suggested that the UK tops the 'drugs league' in Europe with 37.5 per cent of 15–16-year-olds having used cannabis (and 10 per cent of adults). At the same time only 1.5 per cent of 15–16-year-olds claimed to have tried cocaine. Given its price, one might be surprised that so many of this age group made this claim, just as one might not be surprised at all that the vast majority of people admitting to use said they had snorted and not smoked it (or injected it, but that route, fortunately, seems pretty much gone forever).

After a long absence, cocaine came back on the agenda in the 1970s with a huge increase, in the USA, of middle-class use followed rapidly by the 'crack epidemic' among the poor of the 1980s. In Britain, as usual about fifteen years behind trends or fashions in the United States, it has become an increasingly bigger issue since the mid-1980s. But it has been in the 1990s that cocaine has begun to burgeon here as the adult drug of choice, excluding marijuana use, which is now so commonplace as to be routine. It is this author's belief that, after the cannabis issue resolves itself as it surely will in the coming decade, the next furore will erupt over the very widespread use of cocaine. If this occurs the irony will not be lost on historians: a hundred years will have passed since this issue presented itself in similar ways, almost exclusively in the USA. There they took the punitive, prohibitive view, moving first to ban its use and then to stamp down on anyone who might have tried to go on obtaining it. In many ways, cocaine was the drug which started the universal highway to prohibition we are all stuck with, at a huge and growing cost.

This book is about the cultural history of coca and cocaine. It is published as there is another moral panic about cocaine, as well as drugs in general, and at a time when the new President of the United States is likely to start a whole new drugs war. In Britain we have got ourselves in a terrible muddle about drugs, from the absolutes of the Labour government, apparently implacably opposed to even opening a debate on the subject; to the machinations of the Conservative opposition, torn between a libertarian relaxation on control and more restrictions; and to the flapping of the Lib-Dems, whose instincts may be, well, more liberal. The police, too, are torn between implementing the law and knowing how impossible that often is. All around, there remains uncertainty and doubt, fear and fascination. Behind the current mess is the one group of people who know they want things to stay fiercely prohibitive: professional criminals, who will go on making many lives miserable nearly as fast as they make huge sums of money.

PART ONE

CULTURE CLASHES

1

LEAF OF THE GODS,
FRUIT OF THE DEVIL

FROM THE EARLY SIXTEENTH CENTURY ON, European travellers in ancient Peru were all struck by the constant use of the coca leaf by the natives, be they of noble birth or simple peasants and workers. Ancient Peru covered a vast region of South America: modern Ecuador and Peru itself, as well as parts of Colombia, Bolivia and Chile.

By the time the Spanish Conquistadores arrived on the coast in 1532, the earlier Inca custom of attempting to limit the use of coca to the extended royal family and various officials and other privileged groups had more or less collapsed. The Incas regarded the coca plant as divine, hence their desire to limit its daily use. But chewing the leaf is far, far older than Incan civilisation. From as long ago as 3000 BC tombs have been found with coca leaves inside, and it is more than possible that the first use was as long ago as 20,000 BC, when hunter-gatherers moved into the Andean region. Speculative research has suggested that these early settlers might have first tried the leaves after watching animals feeding on them and, subsequently, noticing that these animals became more alert. A similar suggestion has been made for the discovery of coffee by an Ethiopian goat herder who watched his flock eating coffee beans off the bushes and becoming considerably more frisky.

By the time of the Inca, many myths had been invented by earlier cultures to explain the plant's origin; the Inca added more of their own as well as incorporating the others. One of the most popular Inca myths is of a beautiful woman who had been put to death because of her sexual appetite; she was cut to pieces. From these pieces sprang a shrub called *mamacoca*. Her killers then carried the plant in small bags that were only opened once they had had intercourse with a woman. Even today, it is said that the men harvesting the coca crop will seek sex on the eve of the harvest in the belief it will ensure a better crop.

Another myth describes the terrible storm of Khuno, the god of snow and tempest. When the Indians of the Altiplano crossed the mountains and settled in the high valleys of the montana, they found it necessary to set fire to parts of the jungle to make it fit to live in. Khuno was angered by this clearance, because the smoke polluted the peaks. In retaliation he sent down a fierce storm which destroyed everything; the people ran for their lives as the rivers burst their banks. When the farmers returned from the caves they had taken shelter in, they found complete desolation. In searching for food, though, they came across an unknown shrub with brilliant green leaves which they harvested to eat. Immediately they were overwhelmed by a feeling of well-being. Because of this plant – coca – they were able to survive, passing on their knowledge to their descendants.

We generally assume that coca culture – and the term is entirely appropriate, even today – exists solely in and around the Andes. In the Amazon basin, where, as noted before, coca powder is snorted, other myths are used to explain its origin. The Tukanoan Indians of the Colombian Vaupés, for example, say that the sun father was a medicine man who originated the knowledge and power of modern *payés* (medicine men). He had in his navel the powder of *viho*, a powerful narcotic snuff prepared from the bark-resin of trees of the myristicaceous genus, *virola*. A daughter of the Master of Game Animals owned *caapi*, the narcotic plant (*Banisteriopsis caapi*). Pregnant and in great pain, she lay down. An old Indian woman, in an attempt to help her, took hold of her hand and broke off a finger which she kept and guarded in the *maloca*, or roundhouse. A young man then stole the finger, and *caapi* grew from it.

Another daughter of the Master of Game Animals also fell pregnant and, also in pain, lay down. Another old woman came to help, seized the girl's hand and broke off a finger. This she buried. It took root to become the first coca plant. There are many similar legends from a number of tribes of the north-west Amazon about the supernatural and ancient origin of coca. All point to a great antiquity of knowledge and use.

By the time of the Inca, coca was well established as a food and a medicine, and had sacred elements attached to its use. The third Inca emperor, Lloque Yupanqui (*circa* AD 1150), led an army to the montana to search for it. Sometime during his reign he established what is thought to be the first Inca coca plantation at Havisca. Garcillassco de la Vega, writing 350 years later, reported that it was still in production.

After Yupanqui, however, the plant disappears from view – at least as far as the Inca are concerned – until its re-introduction by the Inca Roca 150 years later. But by the fourteenth century the coca plant was in use throughout the empire, from the Amazon Basin, across the Andes, north to modern-day Colombia and south to what is now Chile. The preferred leaf was grown exclusively on the eastern slopes of the Andes in the montanas, but it was grown in many other places too. It was certainly traded extensively. Recently, just how far that trade might have spread has been creating waves in Egyptology, where mummies have been tested for drugs using hair, bone and soft tissue. Expecting to possibly find traces of opium, researchers from the Munich Museum, who conducted the tests, were astonished to find traces of both nicotine and cocaine. Both are new world plants, previously thought not to have reached the old world before 1492 (and the first Columbus voyage). Although tests like these, based on mummies, are uncertain in provenance, similar tests on South American mummies, where coca leaves are present in the graves, show similar levels of coca.

Some of the later Incan emperors held the value of coca to be higher than that of gold, an attitude no doubt lending weight to the argument for restricting its use to the royal family and others deigned important enough. What we can see is that in fact this 'divine plant's' characteristics were well established and integrated in a variety of ways into the lives of millions of people.

The Incan relationship with coca during the reign of Pachacuti was one of *huaca*, a basic concept suggesting residual power in a place, thing or person. A mummy, a stone or a mountain could be *huaca*, and coca was viewed as such. Despite the Incas' insistence that coca was not actually worshipped, it had divine status because it was a means of force and strength for the rulers in Cuzco. Out of this came the restrictions on its use and usages.

Apart from the extended royal family (and this was a very large group), official state messengers (called *chasqui*), whose job it was to pass along information, used coca in their daily work. The *chasqui* were, in effect, exceptional sprinters who, using the coca leaves they carried to give them added stamina, could between them carry messages as far as 150 miles a day. They also moved high-value goods and chattels for the royal family. Fish, caught in the Pacific, could be eaten in Cuzco the following day – 300 miles from the coast and all uphill. Court orators – *yaravecs* – were also allowed its use. These officials were court orators. Using the *quipus* of knotted string, they acted as oral libraries. Part of our continuing lack of knowledge about the detailed history of Incan life has been that the Incas never developed a written language.

The Incan empress was called Mama Coca – an indication of the degree to which Incan civilisation incorporated the coca leaf into its culture. The Incan 'Venus' was represented holding a spray of coca, typifying the powers and fruitfulness of love. On the other hand, convicted thieves were forced to work in the coca plantations, where conditions were harsh. Sacrificial victims – who were revered by the Incas – were almost certainly fed coca leaves to drug them before they were killed. This contrasts greatly with the practice of the Aztecs to the far north, who tore the hearts out of their still-living sacrifices.

So, we know that coca leaves have been chewed in the Andean region of South America since time immemorial. As the nineteenth-century British traveller Clements Markham put it:

> The coca leaf is a great source of comfort and enjoyment to the Peruvian Indian; it is to him what betel is to the Hindoo, kava to the South Sea islander, and tobacco to the rest of mankind; but its use produces invigorating effects which are not possessed by the other stimulants. From the most ancient times the Peruvians have used this beloved leaf, and they still look upon it with feelings of superstitious veneration. In the time of the Incas it was sacrificed to the sun, the Huillac Umu or high priest chewing the leaf during the ceremony; and before the arrival of the Spaniards it was used as the cacao in Mexico, instead of money.

For the Incas, coca was used in any number of religious ceremonies. Every morning as it rose, the sun was greeted with an offering of some food that had been specially prepared, the rest of which served for the priests' breakfast. A fire of specially carved wood was laid; this was kindled at sunrise and the food thrown in, while a priest recited 'Eat this, Lord Sun, and acknowledge thy children.' Later in the day a dark-red llama was sacrificed to the sun, together with some coca. The fragrant, carved wood for the fire was supplied by the Chicha people. Another fire of the same wood was kept constantly burning in a stone brazier near the temple of the sun, and from this all sacrificial fires had to be kindled.

On the first day of each month a ceremony was held in the presence of the emperor and his court, assembled in the Great Square in Cuzco. A hundred selected llamas were brought in and divided among some thirty attendants, three or four to each. Every attendant had one day of the month allotted to him and on this day he brought his animals and sacrificed them. Before the division, all the llamas were ceremonially made to circle the images of the gods four times and dedicated by the High Priest to Viracocha (the eighth Incan emperor – he assumed the title Viracocha the Creator when he ascended the throne) in the name of the sun. These animals were cut into quarters and completely burned in a large fire made of the same carved, scented wood, into which coca, white corn and ground chilli peppers were thrown. The bones that remained were ground to a fine powder and the priests blew a little of this into the air while they recited a short ritual prayer. The remaining powder was stored in a neighbouring building, called the 'Puma's Tail'.

Incan doctors were also known to use coca. If the illness were considered to be the result of a neglect of worship, the doctor made a powder of cornflour of various colours and pulverised seashells and placed it in the patient's hand. The latter blew it in the direction of a *waca* (a kind of sacred shrine; there were thousands of them, ranging from piles of stone to great temples) while reciting a prayer for forgiveness. To the sun he offered some coca and for Viracocha he might put some pieces of gold and silver on the ground. Coca was also occasionally used as a crude anaesthetic. There remains evidence from skulls which have been discovered that it was used in trepanning operations (cutting right into the skull, probably to relieve chronic headache).

After the Spanish conquest in the early 1500s, although the virtues of the coca plant were extolled by the Incas, Garcilassco de le Vega and the Jesuit priest Acosta, many among the Spanish wanted to proscribe its use and to root up the plants. This was because coca had been part of the ancient superstitions of the Incas and because the cultivation of coca took Indians away from other work – notably silver- and gold-mining.

The second council of Lima in 1569, consisting of Catholic bishops from all parts of South America, condemned the use of coca on the grounds that it was a 'useless and pernicious leaf and on account of the belief stated to be entertained by the Indians that the habit of chewing coca gave them strength which is an illusion of the Devil'. But the Spanish governors were torn, because they had rapidly discovered that the Indians worked harder if they had access to coca. There was also the question of taxation, in so far as the local government needed sources of revenue.

The ubiquity of coca was a temptation too great to resist, despite any number of imprecations from the Catholic Church about heathen, if not directly idolatrous, practices. The problem with coca was that it was not an exportable product, unlike tobacco, sugar – or silver. As we shall see, coca leaves deteriorate rapidly under all kinds of adverse conditions, even changes of altitude. But, given the conditions in the silver mines, even King Phillip II of Spain seems to have been convinced that the local use of coca was the only way in which silver could be mined in the rapacious way the Spanish required.

Outside of South America, few knew about the wonder plant or how it was used. Although Amerigo Vespucci had noted Indians in the Caribbean chewing it (another indication of its trading potential) in 1505, very few in Europe could have known about it. Its use was almost exclusively confined to the Indians, although sometimes a Spanish settler would try it. For instance, Garcilassco de la Vega related the following tale:

> I remember a story which I heard in my native land of Peru of a gentleman of rank and honour named Rodrigo Pantoja who travelled from Cuzco to Rimac [Lima] and met a poor Spaniard who was going on foot with a little girl aged two years on his back. The man was known to Pantoja and they thus conversed. 'Why do you go laden thus?' said the knight. The poor man answered that he was unable to hire an Indian to carry the child and for that reason he carried her himself. While he spoke Pantoja looked in his mouth and saw that it was full of coca; and, as the Spaniards abominate all that the Indians eat and drink as though it savoured of idolatry, particularly the chewing of coca which seems to them a low and vile habit, he said: 'It may be as you say but why do you eat coca like an Indian, a thing so hateful to the Spaniards?' The man answered, 'In truth, my lord, I detest it as much as anyone but necessity obliges me to imitate the Indians and keep coca in my mouth; for I would have you know that, if I did not do so I could not carry this burden; while the coca gives me sufficient strength to endure the fatigue.' Pantoja was astonished to hear this and told the story wherever he went.

Eventually Don Fransisco Toledo, Viceroy of Peru, permitted the cultivation of coca with voluntary labour on condition that the Indians were well paid and that care was taken of their health (the valleys in which coca grew were thought to be unhealthy). Given the average way in which Indians were treated by their conquerors, this sounds breathtakingly two-faced to the cynical twenty-first-century ear. Nevertheless, there were 70 ordinances on coca and coca-growing issued by Toledo between 1570 and 1574.

On the taxation issue, Acosta estimated that by 1583 the trade in Potosi – the mining centre – alone was worth half a million dollars. In 1591 an excise duty of 5 per cent was imposed, a tax which, 200 years later, would be yielding two-and-a-half times as much.

Apart from its use by Indians in South America and the occasional Spaniard, the coca leaf was never going to catch on much in Europe. Much like Qhat today, the Yemeni version of coca still legally bought and sold in the markets of east London, coca chewing is an art deeply embedded in Indian culture. The Conquistadores disparaged just about everything they saw in South America and although coca leaves were brought back to Europe early on, we can be fairly certain it was as a curiosity. The rejection by the Spanish of coca also stemmed from its bitter taste, but the greater revulsion would have been that it was popular among 'pagans' who, despite their number, had allowed themselves to be conquered by just a few hundred Europeans.

The first known attempt in Europe to categorise coca comes from Nicolas Monardes, a doctor from Seville who lived in the sixteenth century. Monardes almost certainly saw the plant from his description, a translation of which, into Latin, is usually quoted as the earliest reference to coca in Europe. The Kew library in London has an English translation with the title *Joyful News out of the Newe Founde Worlde, wherein is declared the Virtues of Herbes, Treez, Oyales, Plantes and Stones*. Monardes wrote:

> This plant Coca has been celebrated for many years among the Indians, and they sow and cultivate it with much care and industry, because they all apply it daily to their use and pleasure. It is indeed of the height of two outstretched arms, its leaves somewhat like myrtle, but larger and more succulent and green (and they have, as it were, drawn in the middle of them another leaf of a similar shape); its fruit collected together in a cluster, which like myrtle fruit, becomes red when ripening and of the same size, and when quite ripe it is black in

colour. When the time of the harvest arrives, they are collected in baskets with other things to make them dry, that they may be better preserved, and may be carried to other places.

The Jesuit priest Joseph de Acosta arrived in Peru in 1570 after an Atlantic passage which, he caustically remarks, 'would have been more rapid if the mariners had made more sail'. He travelled from Lima over the Andes to join Viceroy Toledo, with whom he visited every province. At the higher altitudes the party suffered from severe bouts of what we now know to be Acute Mountain Sickness, from which a few cups of coca tea might have saved them. Father Acosta, though, was an intelligent and learned man who was not overburdened with prejudices. His *Natural History of the Indies* is still a classic work. He has provided an early and fascinating account of coca:

> They bring it commonly from the valleys of the Andes, where there is an extreme heat and where it rains continually the most part of the year, wherein the Indians endure much labour and pain to entertain it, and often many die. They go from the Sierra and colde places to till and gather them in the valleys; and therefore there has been great question and diversity of opinion among learned men whether it were more expedient to pull up these trees or let them grow, but in the end they remained.
>
> The Indians esteemed it much, and in the time of the Incas it was not lawful for any of the common people to use this Coca without licence from the government . . . They say it gives them great courage and is very pleasing to them. Many grave men hold this as a superstition and a mere imagination. For my part, and to speak the truth, I persuade not myself that it is an imagination, but contrariwise I think it works and gives force and courage to the Indians, for we see effects which cannot be attributed to imagination, so as to go some days without meat, but only a handful of Coca, and other like effects. The sauce wherewith they do eat this Coca is proper enough, whereof I have tasted, and it is like the taste of leather. The Indians mix it with the ashes of bones, burnt and beat into powder, or with lime, as others affirme, which seemeth to them pleasing and of good taste, and they say it doeth them much good.

In the event, it was through Holland that the coca plant came back to Europe. In 1630 the Dutch took control of Pernambuco on Brazil's north-east coast and held onto it for twenty-four years before the Portuguese re-claimed it. The Dutch settlers sent a stream of plants back, particularly to the University of Leiden with its famous botanical garden. Monardes's text on coca and other medicinal plants had been translated into Latin (still the lingua franca in Europe at that time) by the first director of this garden, Charles de L'Ecluse, in 1574. But it remains unclear whether any of the people associated with written texts on coca had any direct access to the plant or, more crucially, the seeds.

Coca leaves do travel badly and any samples brought, by any route, to Europe would have been unlikely to yield any of the effects described by travellers. A further problem was that as the leaf was so popular among the natives in Peru, little would have been left over from each crop for export. So coca leaves, although discussed and written about – the English poet Cowley even wrote a poem entitled 'A Legend of Coca' in 1662 – outside South America, they remained a fabulous idea rather than a reality. It would take a seismic shift in European culture to ensure a re-discovery of coca, just as it would later take a seismic shift in science to reveal the secrets hidden inside this apparently innocuous plant.

2

EXOTICA AND ENLIGHTENMENT

THE EXPANSION OF EUROPEAN INTEREST in the wider world, fuelled by a desire to find a sea-route to India and the Far East, opened up a cornucopia of far more worth than mere gold and silver, or exotic spices. Between the sixteenth and the eighteenth centuries, any number of new foodstuffs and other consumables arrived in Europe, borne on the wings of exploration. Among them were tea, tobacco, coffee and cacao (the basis of chocolate and cocoa).

The coca leaf, as we have seen, fared badly against these other potentially addictive substances. It required the addition of alcohol (for reasons which were only recognised a decade ago) or, in a paler imitation, caffeine and carbon dioxide to make it into a form of soft drink. The leaves were not as robust as, say, tea, and their cocaine content rapidly deteriorated if they were not packed and shipped in exactly the right way. As no one knew what the active ingredient was and others doubted it existed at all, coca would remain the Cinderella on this list well into the nineteenth century.

For a twenty-first-century audience tobacco is now a controversial item, condemned for its side effects but still a potent drug, in use worldwide. Tobacco was observed in use by Christopher Columbus in 1492, on his first voyage. It began to be shipped back to Europe a little later from both the Caribbean and Brazil; the oldest European written reference to it is thought to have been made by Rembertus Dodonaeus in 1554. Jean Nicot (who gave his name to nicotine) described it when he served as French Ambassador to Portugal in 1560. Its rapid spread dismayed nearly as many as it pleased. King James VI of Scotland and I of England was among those disgusted by its use. But the sailors and soldiers who first took up smoking, purely through proximity to it (and who, worldwide, remain among its heaviest users), helped popularise the habit. The English, who were to become the chief growers and distributors, were using clay pipes in London as early as 1580. They started early on to re-export tobacco to Holland, Norway and even Russia.

Cacao was brought back to England by Columbus, who would have observed local Indians drinking it as a spicy concoction called *xocoatl*, but the beans were discarded. It was Hernan Cortes, conqueror of the Aztecs, who showed the Portuguese and Spanish how to prepare the beans for drinking, a secret kept in the Iberian peninsula of Spain and Portugal for the whole of the sixteenth century. Coffee came into Europe from the Ottoman Empire, probably after emerging from Ethiopia and spreading throughout Arabia. It was being drunk in Cairo twenty years before Pizarro discovered the Incas' use of the coca leaf in 1532, but it was a hundred years before coffee came to Italy (through Venice, which was then a power in its own right) and thence to France overland. More or less at the same time, it was being shipped into northern Europe by sea.

Finally, tea, which had been used in Asia since antiquity, arrived courtesy of the Dutch East India Company some time early in the seventeenth century. The earliest written references in the British East India Company may be found close to this time. It was well into this century before serious orders (in the sense of quantities) for tea were placed.

Yet all these substances, much like the coca leaf in the nineteenth and twentieth centuries, went through a similar process; all were at first classified as purely medicinal. It is important to realise that Europe was emerging from the Middle Ages, a period we now know was not anti-scientific as such, but mired and trammelled by theological disputes of the most extreme kind; these frequently put science in the same category as works of the Devil. This included what very basic (and usually utterly wrong) medicine did exist.

The doctors of the time were desperate for new measures. (This would remain a truth well into the twentieth century.) They sought new methods of understanding in a 'dark age'. The pursuit of better scientific methods was aided by the Age of Discovery, which provided evidence of a much more complex universe than had been hitherto imagined, let alone mapped. But to be interested in either medicine or science was to court disaster as often as it was to court fame and fortune. Given the paucity of materials, it is not surprising that much of the exotica transported from the New World ended up with the doctors of the time.

Tobacco was early on considered a disinfectant, a view which lingered until the twentieth century in some far-flung medical outposts. Others said it was good to use against hunger, thirst or insomnia. Similarly, the Aztecs used the cacao plant for dysentery, diarrhoea and as an aphrodisiac (a view most definitely still in the minds of twenty-first-century advertising agencies). Finally, both tea and coffee were widely prescribed by doctors – a parallel may be seen in the use of tea to treat mild conditions of shock in and around twentieth-century medicine.

At the same time, the introduction of all of these substances excited controversy. Governments – as in the present day – remained torn between their desire to control and their anxiety to raise revenue; in the end, they frequently used the latter to enforce the former. Attempts of various kinds were made to ban tobacco (an order prohibiting its use in any part of the Spanish empire was made in 1575). In England, its use by ordinary people as a drug was thought to produce laziness and a nose for rebellion, both at the same time. Logic has rarely come into debates about drug use.

James VI and I famously published his *A Counterblast to Tobacco* in 1604, after therapy from his own surgeon (perhaps the first recorded case of a cure for smoking). In his anonymously published pamphlet (although the secret was soon out), his new-found hatred for tobacco surges off the page:

> He that taketh tobacco saith he cannot leave it, it doth bewitch him; even so, the pleasures of the world make men loath to leave them, they are for the most part so enchanted with them; and further, besides all this, it is like hell in the very substance of it, for it is a stinking loathsome thing; and so is hell.

Rather than ban it, even after this diatribe, James increased taxes on it – by a mere 4,000 per cent.

A few years later, despairing of finding anything to grow, the new settlers of the east coast Virginian colony turned to tobacco as their possible saviour. The flavour of this tobacco suited contemporary English tastes; the rest is too well known to repeat, save that by the end of his reign James VI and I, far from ending the habit of smoking, found that he was perforce the arbiter of the quality of the tobacco in widespread use. Adulteration of tobacco had arisen as the direct result of the huge tax increases he had imposed. (A similar case could be made for the legalisation and licensing of most current illicit drugs. This would prevent both smuggling and adulteration, as well as providing additional taxation, including that for policing the system. If any such changes were to be made, it would probably be the taxation argument which would sway governments.)

Cacao, transformed into cocoa, got off rather lightly compared with tobacco, but nonetheless was the cause of a long-standing debate over whether it inflamed passions. Tea had to wait until John Wesley, Methodism and the eighteenth century before it came under a sustained attack. The nub of Wesley's argument was, once more, that it led to indolence. He seems to have missed the point: in the poor's use of tea, they were only emulating their 'betters' in the country estates and town and city mansion houses, for whom indolence was reaching an art form. Coffee, meanwhile, had been vilified by large numbers of Islamic religious leaders for the same reasons and also raised a spectre of political debate in Europe. Curiously enough, in Restoration England of the 1660s and 1670s, it was women who petitioned to have coffee banned, suggesting its ingestion led both to domestic disorder and sexual inactivity in their men.

Yet over time, and we are talking about hundreds of years rather than decades, each of these controversial substances has become a commonplace along with a very wide range of others, including many herbs and spices (like saffron or cinnamon). Mixed in with all of these – inextricably intertwined – is alcohol in its many forms, creating a series of moral panics throughout history in its own right. Perhaps among the best known of these is the eighteenth-century panic in England about gin, on which subject we still have the magnificent paintings of William Hogarth.

On the periphery of these seething concerns are both cannabis and opium, confined mainly to medical use but, as the eighteenth century moved into the nineteenth, breaking out into wider society. The coca leaf remained the most peripheral of all, hardly a ripple on the surface of debate. There were few exceptions. In 1708 the Dutch physician, Herman Boerhaave (the director of the 'physik garden' at Leiden, it will be recalled) published the *Institutiones Medicae*, in which he reviewed various medicinal herbs. Coca had a prominent place although, mysteriously, it was missing from his *Materia medica* published in 1755. This implies that coca was not grown in the Leiden University garden and that, once again, accounts were secondhand. All this was to change as the eighteenth century progressed.

The Enlightenment of the eighteenth century had as big an impact as the Renaissance on the future progression of Europe; perhaps its greatest impact may be seen in the sciences, but its processes also had a profound effect on the way people in Europe thought politically and economically. In politics, it led to both the American and the French Revolutions; economically it can be seen to be intertwined with the English Industrial Revolution; scientifically, it created an atmosphere in which the spirit of inquiry was never again to be constrained.

In terms of the history of both the coca leaf and cocaine it meant that, for the first time in general European history, men (and a few notable women) would look at the natural world to seek answers to a huge range of questions, without imposing an entrenched philosophy or theology upon whatever results might be found. The progression of the ideas central to the Enlightenment was patchy, mixed in with the vagaries associated with the times. There were constant setbacks, constant tugs toward older and less rational thinking. There were, as well, economic considerations and it ought never to be forgotten that science – in this case botany – was pressed openly into the service of profit.

The expeditions which began to leave the shores of Europe at this time headed off in all directions, but mostly to South America, long colonised by the Portuguese and Spanish, whose empires were by now in long decline. There were established trade routes and the New World continued to exercise a magnetic pull on Europeans. The expeditions were also the direct result of the lifting of the Spanish monopoly on trading with South America in 1700. The new explorations were not based on the concept of conquest at all, but on a subtle blend of a genuine spirit of inquiry mixed with the possibility of real profit. There was, too, an interest in solving that greatest of navigation puzzles, the longitude question, with all the benefits for improving trade (by making it safer) that that would bring.

The French Academy sponsored a major expedition to the new world in 1735, typical of its time, being based on a scientific rivalry between France and England over the shape of the earth (there are shades of the Russo-American Space Race here). Without delving too deeply, the argument was between Newton's theory that the earth was an oblate (flattened at the poles) spheroid and the French astronomer royal Cassini's belief that it was a prolate (lengthened at the poles) spheroid. To settle the matter two parties were sent by the French, one to the Arctic and the other to the Equator, to measure the meridian of an arc of one degree of latitude (if Newton were right, an arc of one degree of latitude ought to be slightly longer in the Arctic: it was).

Despite objections from his Council of the Indies, Philip V of Spain allowed the expedition to Peru (although two Spanish officers went along with the French to keep an eye on them). The South American half sailed on 16 May 1735; it was led by Charles-Marie de La Condamine, a friend of Voltaire, the latter perhaps the one individual most associated with the Enlightenment. Unwittingly, it sailed into another kind of history.

Among the crew was a French botanist called Joseph de Jussieu, who, in his travels in South America, came across coca leaves. De Jussieu had a more prominent cousin, Antoine. He eventually managed to ship a consignment of coca leaves which he had collected to Antoine, when the first were destroyed after thieves broke open the dockside crates containing the leaves thinking they concealed valuables. (In their frustration they tipped the crates of leaves into the sea; Joseph, upon hearing of this loss, apparently had a nervous breakdown.) Back in Paris Antoine examined them, then gave them to the Museum of Natural History, where they were looked at by Carl Von Linnaeus, the botanical and zoological classifier *sans pareil*. Later, Lamarck, another of the century's great classifiers, examined them. The coca plant appeared in Lamarck's encyclopedia of 1786 as *Erythroxylon coca*; this did turn out to be a coca plant, but not of the variety used by the Indians, nor the kind usually exported from the nineteenth century onward.

The La Condamine expedition, whose principal botanic success was not coca but rubber and quinine (from the cinchona tree), begat many more. In 1801 Friedrich Heinrich Alexander Baron von Humbolt, perhaps the greatest of all polymathic explorers (certainly the opinion of Charles Darwin), came across the Peruvian province of Popayan, where he observed the locals chewing coca. He also discovered their use of lime (calcium oxide) while chewing the leaves and mistakenly believed that it was the lime which was the active ingredient, not the coca. (He made the same mistake with the use of betel nuts in Asia.) Baron von Humbolt was convinced that this was why Europeans had failed to get coca to work for them: they had just shoved the leaf into their mouths, failing to appreciate the value of the lime.

Humbolt's view hardly mattered. A spirit of inquiry was beginning to develop, however misplaced, which no longer dismissed any native experience of local flora and fauna as beyond the pale. Attitudes towards the exotic had aleady begun to change. The experiences explored by the Romantic movement in art and literature were expanding far beyond the mundane. De Quincey's *Confessions of an English Opium Eater* was published in 1821, but the book discusses the issue of a long-term habit. De Quincey regularly took massive quantities of laudanum (the liquid form of opium). He was a contemporary and friend of Coleridge, who was also well versed in drug use, bending it, as others would do right up to the present day, to his own literary purposes. This period would herald the great economic and technological expansion of the second industrial revolution and, in parallel, the world of art and letters would undertake its own forms of progress, often in direct opposition to the ravages of an industrial and alienated society.

But if the use of opium was to become a very general problem as the century progressed, helped in some part by de Quincey's rhapsodic and at times delirious prose, coca was to continue to be surrounded by mystique. Its physical distance yet tantalising presence was made more intriguing by its association with the past. Thus, in 1817, a letter to the *Gentleman's Magazine* in London suggested that:

> While not yet fully acquainted with the secret with which the Incas sustain power, it is certain that they have that secret and put it in practice. They masticate coca and undergo the greatest fatigue without any injury to health or bodily vigour. They want neither butcher nor brewer, nor distiller, nor fuel nor culinary utensils. No, if Professor Davy [inventor of the miners' safety lamp] will apply his thoughts to the subject, there are thousands even in this happy land who will pour their blessings upon him if he discover a temporary anti-famine, or substitute food free from all inconvenience of weight, bulk and expense, and by which any person might be enabled, like the Peruvian Indian, to live and labour in health and good spirits for a month now and then without eating.

Whilst speculation like this continued in Europe, others travelled to see for themselves. Among them was a German doctor, J.J. Von Tschudi, who was in Peru between 1838 and 1842. It is worth quoting Von Tschudi at length. Despite being written 160 years ago, his is a very contemporaneous outline of coca and its uses, largely devoid of any of our current cultural prejudice. He writes:

> The dwellings of the shepherds are built in the same rude style which characterises all the huts in the Puna [the high altitude region where

people suffered from AMS], and they impress the European traveller with a very unfavourable notion of the intelligence of the people . . . Internally these huts present miserable pictures of poverty and uncleanliness . . . On dirty sheepskins spread on the ground, sit the Indian and his wife; listlessly munching their coca . . .

With respect to silver-mining he writes:

The Indian labours with a degree of patient industry, which it would be vain to expect the European workman similarly circumstanced . . . Content with wretched food, and with still more wretched lodging, the *hapire* [miner] goes through his hard day's work, partaking of no refreshment but coca, and at the end of the week, he possibly finds himself in possession of a dollar.

As to the coca plant and its cultivation, Tschudi noted that:

The coca is a shrub about six feet in height with bright green leaves and white blossoms. The latter are succeeded by small scarlet berries. It is raised from the seed, in garden beds called *almazigas*. When the young shoots are one-and-a-half or two feet high they are removed to regularly laid-out coca fields [*cocales*] where they are planted at the distance of about three spans from each other. The coca requires humidity; therefore, during the first year or two after it is planted in the fields maize is sown between the *matas* or young shoots to screen them from the too great influence of the sun. When the leaves are ripe, that is to say when on being bent they crack or break off, the gathering commences. The leaves are stripped from the branches, a task usually performed by women, and it requires great care lest the tender leaves and young twigs should be injured. In some districts the Indians are so careful in gathering the coca that, instead of stripping off the leaves, they cut them from the stem by making an incision with their nails.

The plant thus rendered leafless is soon again overgrown with verdant foliage. After being gathered the leaves are spread out on coarse woollen cloths and dried in the sun. The colour of the leaves when dried is a pale green. The drying is an operation which likewise demands great care and attention, for if the leaves imbibe damp they become dark-coloured and then they sell for a much lower price than when they are green. The dry coca is finely packed in woollen sacks and covered with sand. These sacks are of various sizes and colours, in different parts of the Montanas. In Huanaco they are grey or black, and when filled weigh from 75 to 80 pounds. In Vitoc they are grey or white and contain 150 pounds. In Huanta and Anco they are small in size and black or brown in colour and contain merely one aroba. In the Montanas of Urubamba, Calca and Paucartambo the coca leaves are put into small baskets called *cestos* and covered with sand. Great care is also requisite in the carriage of the coca for if damp be allowed to penetrate the sack the leaves become hot or, as the natives express it, *se calientan*, and are thereby rendered useless. [This had been one of the major problems in the transporting of still-active coca leaves more or less anywhere outside the region, where good practice was known, and especially back to Europe.]

He observed in detail the way in which Indians masticated the coca. Each individual carried a leathern pouch called a *huallqui* or the *chuspa* and a small flask gourd called the *ishcupuru*. The pouch contained a supply of coca leaves and the gourd was filled with pulverised unslaked lime. Usually four times, but never less than three times a day, the Indians stopped working in order to masticate coca (which they told him they called *chacchar* or *acullicar*). To enable them do this, some of the coca leaves, the stalks having been carefully picked off, were masticated until they formed a small ball, or *acullico*. A thin slip of damp wood was then pushed into the *ishcupuru*, or gourd. When this was drawn out, some of the powdered lime stuck to it.

> The *acculico* or ball of masticated coca leaves is, whilst still lying in the mouth, punctured with this slip of wood, until the lime mixing with it gives a proper relish, and the abundant flow of saliva thus excited is partly expectorated and partly swallowed. When the ball ceases to emit juice, it is thrown away, and a new one is formed by the mastication of a fresh mouthful of coca leaves.

He added,

> The application of the unslaked lime demands some precaution, for if

it comes in direct contact with the lips and gums, it causes very painful burning.

Tschudi also said that during a tiring ride across the altiplano where, as he put it, 'owing to the cold wind' he experienced difficulty in breathing, his guide recommended he chew coca, assuring him that he would experience a great relief. He lent Tschudi his *huallqui*, but 'owing to my awkward manner of using it, I cauterised my lips so severely that I did not venture on a second experiment'.

The flavour of the coca was not unpleasant, Tschudi thought, though:

It is slightly bitter, aromatic and similar to the worst kind of green tea. When mixed with the ashes of the musa root it is somewhat piquant, and more pleasant to European palates than it is without that addition. The smell of the fresh dried leaves in a mass is almost overpowering; but this smell entirely goes when they are packed in the sacks. All who masticate coca have a very bad breath, pale lips, and gums, greenish and stumpy teeth, and an ugly black mark at the angles of the mouth. An invererate *coquero*, or coca chewer, is known at first glance. His unsteady gait, his yellow-coloured skin, his dim and sunken eyes encircled by a purple ring, his quivering lips and his general apathy, all bear evidence of the baneful effects of the coca juice when taken in excess.

Tschudi said that all the mountain Indians were addicted, more or less, to the practice of masticating coca. Each man consumed on average between an ounce (25 grams) and an ounce-and-a-half per day (40 grams) and, on festival days, about double that quantity. The owners of the mines and plantations allowed their labourers to suspend their work three times a day for the *chacchar*, which usually occupied upwards of a quarter of an hour. 'After that they smoked a paper cigar, which they alleged crowned the zest of the coca mastication. He who indulged for a time in the use of the coca found it difficult, indeed almost impossible to stop.'

In Lima, he noted that there were people of 'high respectability' who were in the habit of retiring daily to a private apartment for the purpose of masticating coca. They could not do this openly, because among refined Peruvians the *chacchar* was looked upon as a low and vulgar practice befitting only the labouring Indians. Yet Europeans occasionally allowed themselves to fall into this habit; Tschudi knew two in Lima, one an Italian and the other a Biscayan, who were confirmed *coqueros* in the strictest sense of the word. In Cerro de Pasco he found societies where Englishmen were members, which met on certain evenings just for the *chacchar*. In these clubs, instead of lime or ashes, sugar was served along with the coca leaves. A member of one of these clubs told him that on the few first trials the sugar was found 'very agreeable, but that afterwards the palate required some more pungent ingredient'.

Tschudi believed that the way coca worked was similar to that of narcotics administered in small doses. Its effects might be compared to those arising from opium. He wrote:

> I have already noticed the consequences resulting from drinking the decoction of the *datura* [a drink made from the red thorn apple, which appeared first to stupify and then convulse the user]. In the inveterate *coquero* similar symptoms are observable, but in a mitigated degree. I may mention one circumstance attending the use of coca which appears hitherto to have escaped notice: it is, that after the mastication of a great quantity of coca the eye seems unable to bear light, and there is a marked distension of the pupil. I have also noticed this peculiarity of the eye in one who had drunk a strong extract of the infusion of coca leaves. In the effects consequent on the use of opium and coca there is this distinction; that coca, when taken even in the utmost excess, never causes a total alienation of the mental powers or induces sleep; but, like opium, it excites the sensibility of the brain, and the repeated excitement, occasioned by its intemperate use after a series of years, wears out mental vigour and activity.

He observed that Indians who regularly masticated coca required little food and could do arduous work for long periods with apparent ease. They ascribed the most extraordinary qualities to the coca, even believing that it might be used entirely as a substitute for food. He argued:

> I am clearly of the opinion that the moderate use of coca is not merely innoxious, but that it may even be very conducive to health. In support of this conclusion, I may refer to the numerous examples of longevity among Indians who, almost from the age of boyhood, have been in the

habit of masticating coca three times a day, and who in the course of their lives have consumed no less than 2,700 pounds (over one tonne of the leaves), yet, nevertheless, enjoy perfect health. (I allude here to individuals [and such cases are by no means singular] who have attained the great age of 130. Supposing these Indians to have begun to masticate coca at ten years old, and calculate their daily consumption as a minimum at one ounce, the result is the consumption of 27 hundredweight in 120 years.)

The food of the Indians at that time consisted almost exclusively of vegetables, especially roasted maize and barley converted into flour by crushing. Tschudi said:

> The continued use of this farinaceous food occasions severe obstructions which the well-known aperient qualities of the coca counteract, and many serious diseases are thereby prevented. That the coca is in the highest degree nutritious is a fact beyond dispute. The incredible fatigues endured by the Peruvian infantry, with very spare diet, but with regular use of coca; the labourious toil of the Indian miner, kept up, under similar circumstances, throughout a long series of years; certainly afford sufficient ground for attributing to the coca leaves, not a quality of mere temporary stimulus, but a powerful nutritive principle.

Similar use of coca and similar claims are, of course, still made to this day by Andean Indians, for whom these descriptions would be perfectly clear as they apply to their daily lives.

Tschudi ends his long account of coca-chewing with this:

> By the Peruvian Indians the coca plant is regarded as something sacred and mysterious, and it sustained an important part in the religion of the Incas. In all ceremonies, whether religious or warlike, it was introduced for producing smoke at the great offerings, or as the sacrifice itself. During divine worship the priests chewed coca leaves, and unless they were supplied with them, it was believed that the favour of the Gods could not be propitiated. It was also deemed necessary that the supplicator for divine grace should approach the

priests with an *acullico* in his mouth. It was believed that any business undertaken without the benediction of coca leaves could not prosper; and to the shrub itself worship was rendered.

During an interval of more than 300 years Christianity has not been able to subdue the deep-rooted idolatry; for everywhere we find traces of belief in the mysterious power of this plant. The excavators in the mines of Cerro de Pasco throw masticated coca on hard veins of metal, in the belief that it softens the ore, and renders it more easy to work. The origin of this custom is easily explained, when it is recollected that in the time of the Incas it was believed that the Coyas, or the deities of metals, rendered the mountains impenetrable, if they were not propitiated by the odour of coca. The Indians, even at the present time, put coca leaves into the mouths of dead persons, to secure to them a favourable reception on their entrance into another world, and when a Peruvian Indian on a journey falls in with a mummy, he, with timid reverence, presents to it some coca leaves as his pious offering.

Dr Von Tschudi's account is remarkable for its lucidity and the way in which it addresses most of the issues still extant today over whether Andean Indian culture should be preserved in full or whether the Indians of today need to be weaned off coca. But, almost as soon as he published, he was under attack by another German, Edward Poeppig, who had earlier been in modern-day Peru as well as modern-day Chile. On the other side of the spectrum he had suggested 'the practice of chewing the leaf is attendant with the most pernicious consequences, producing an intoxication like that of opium. As indulgence is repeated the appetite for it increases and the power of resistance diminishes until at last death relieves the miserable victim.'

A more balanced picture was painted by Clements Markham, another great Victorian explorer and the man who was to get the cinchona tree transplanted to India (via Kew Gardens) thus saving countless lives from malaria. Markham, who published *Travels in Peru and India* in 1862, estimated that around eight million people were using coca when he was there. He sampled it, too:

> I chewed coca, not constantly, but very frequently, from the day of my departure from Sandia, and, besides the agreeable soothing feeling it

produced, I found that I could endure long abstinence from food with less inconvenience than I should otherwise have felt, and it enabled me to ascend precipitous mountainsides with a feeling of lightness and elasticity and without losing breath.

He added:

The latter quality ought to recommend its use to members of the Alpine Club, and to walking tourists in general, though the sea-voyage would probably cause the leaves to lose much of their virtue. To the Peruvian Indians, however, who can procure it within a few weeks of its being picked, the coca is a solace which is easily procured, which affords great enjoyment, and which has a most beneficial effect.

Another Englishman, Richard Spruce from Yorkshire, journeyed to South America in 1849. There he collected thousands of plant samples, among them coca plants, which he found had migrated through cultivation down from the Andes to the Amazon basin, where it was known as *ipadu*. He brought coca leaves back to Europe and, by one account, some of these leaves reached Germany and raised the interest of chemists there.

By now, belief that there was some active ingredient in coca was growing, along with a desire to isolate this unknown ingredient. In 1855, the German chemist Gaedecke isolated a strange-smelling oily liquor now known to be *hygrine*, one of the alkaloids in the coca leaf. He published the results in *Archives de Pharmacie*, where he goes on to describe that further refinement led to needle-like crystals: he called these *erythroxyline* – cocaine. But Gaedecke did not get the credit for the isolation of cocaine, because his experiment could not be duplicated. More than probably this was due to the quality, or lack of it, of the leaves available to researchers in Europe. It was the same old problem: the leaves did not travel well and they were, in any case, badly packed.

It would take the Austrian *Novara* expedition of 1858 to provide the requisite consignment of leaf. The task, getting the right quality as well as quantity of leaf, was performed by Dr Karl Scherzer. But he only did so after Friedrich Wohler, a pharmacist from Gottingen whom Dr Von Tschudi had interested in coca, specifically asked him to get hold of sufficient quantities of fresh leaf to experiment on. Dr Scherzer obtained about 14kg – quite probably the largest amount ever to reach a European laboratory at that time. When they arrived Wohler looked for a student to undertake the experiments; he lighted upon a young, gifted chemist called Albert Niemann, who was looking for a subject for his doctorate.

3

DIVINE PLANT, DANGEROUS GROUND

INTEREST IN THE ALKALOIDS IN LEAF COCA was growing. In 1857 came more experiments, this time in New York by a Dr Percy who claimed to have isolated crystals of what he also called cocaine (there is no evidence that either Gaedecke or Percy knew of the other's work). Percy read a paper at the New York Academy of Medicine in which he too described the anaesthetic properties noted by Gaedecke. But the laurel leaf of discovery was about to be snatched by another man.

When Albert Niemann began work on coca leaves in 1859, he first reviewed all the literature he could find about the subject. Then, working with the high-yield Bolivian leaf provided by Scherzer, he began his laboratory experiments to establish the truth about these increasingly interesting leaves. The method he finally lighted upon was this: first, he saturated some leaves in 85 per cent alcohol with a trace of sulphuric acid. Then he distilled the alcohol and found that he had a syrupy mass. From this, he separated a resin which he treated with sodium carbonate. An alkaloidal substance was then isolated by repeated shaking with ether. The ether was distilled, leaving white crystals, which Niemann also called cocaine. He published *On a New Organic Base in the Coca Leaves* in March 1860. Niemann described cocaine as 'colourless transparent prisms . . . Its solutions have an alkaline reaction, a bitter taste, promote the flow of saliva and *leave a peculiar numbness, followed by a sense of cold when applied to the tongue*' [my italics].

Niemann's discovery was taken notice of much more readily than those of Gaedecke and Percy, not least because Carl Wohler, his sponsor, was a leading chemist and the work emanating from his laboratory was generally accepted. The commercial chemist company, Merck of Darmstadt, began to produce small amounts of purified cocaine each year from this date (no more than 50 grammes or a couple of ounces). It is fairly clear that Merck manufactured cocaine in order to maintain their reputation as a comprehensive supplier of the growing number of alkaloids on the market. However this small quantity meant that prices remained exceptionally high, which may well have put off many researchers from further experiments with the pure heart of the coca leaf. A few tried using it; all kept missing the immediately obvious – that it had a local anaesthetic effect. Frederick Schroff, in 1862, thought that cocaine's after-effects (in his case, a deep depression) more than outweighed its initial benefit of making a person feel cheerful, so much so that he warned against any use of it at all.

Wilhelm Lossen went on in the next year to discover its chemical formula. Later still, other chemists succeeded in isolating and categorising the other alkaloids present in the formula, although they have been little studied even to this day. The impact of cocaine remained muted. On the other hand, that of the coca leaf was to be trumpeted across Europe and beyond.

The reason may be traced to the marketing genius of Angelo Mariani, a Corsican chemist, who, in 1863, apparently unaware of Niemann's discovery of cocaine, patented a concoction of coca extract and Bordeaux wine. Mariani was assiduous to the point of obsession in the promotion of his invention, as we shall shortly see. Vin Mariani began to sweep across Europe and then America, eventually becoming one of the most popular patent medicines of its era. The coca leaf was still hard to come by, but better methods of transport, combined with an ever-increasing interest in exotic plants and their extracts, made it available.

Nineteenth-century writers on the subject of coca extract and cocaine are sometimes vague about which it is they are referring to, or have themselves experimented with. It was not until the mid-1880s that cocaine came clearly to dominate the agenda. By then it was becoming confused with morphine, another difficulty which would (and still does) bedevil the issue, as morphine is a narcotic, cocaine a stimulant. By the mid-nineteenth century, morphine addiction was becoming one of the great scourges of the developed world, one which would continue until being superseded in every sense by heroin.

The story of coca and cocaine during this time takes on many of the aspects of one of the most startling works of fiction of the late nineteenth century, *Doctor Jeykll and Mr Hyde* by Robert Louis Stevenson. The leaves of the coca plant were given a similar persona as that of the good doctor by the public and scientific perception of them. Cocaine, the stronger, wilder and more demonic *alter ego* may be compared to Mr Hyde, at first creating every appearance of ecstatic *joie de vivre* but rapidly descending into bedlam. It is all the more powerful a metaphor when the reader realises that, in all probability, Robert Louis Stevenson wrote *Dr Jeykll and Mr Hyde* while taking cocaine.

Coca leaves continued to dominate the agenda for some decades after cocaine had been isolated. Paolo Mantegazza, the Italian neurologist, had written a powerfully argued case for the use of coca in 1859. His essay was later to find a particular resonance with Sigmund Freud, later the single most important advocate of the unrestricted use not of coca but pure cocaine. Mantegazza was certainly lyrical about coca:

> I prefer a life of ten years with coca to one of a hundred thousand without it. It seemed to me that I was separated from the whole world, and I beheld the strangest images, most beautiful in colour and in form, that can be imagined.

He was still sufficiently in control of himself to point out that overuse of coca could cause emaciation, digestive complaints and 'moral depravity'. But equally, he strongly recommended it for toothache, digestive disorders and, critically, neurasthenia. Today, neurasthenia is not recognised as an illness at all; but, as with hysteria, it was a very common nineteenth-century diagnosis of chronic mental illness, affecting both men and women. It was this concatenation of symptoms (in himself as well as others) that Freud was investigating when *he* first lighted upon cocaine twenty-five years later.

Not all the interest in or developments over coca and cocaine took place in Europe, or even North America. In 1868 the surgeon-general of the Peruvian army, Tomas Moreno y Mais, experimented with cocaine and announced that it provided 'some of the most blessed moments of my life'. It is probably of some significance that many early experimenters with both coca and cocaine described their experiences in religious terms. But Mais also stumbled onto the one obvious physical effect. Experimenting on frogs, he asked: 'Could one utilise it as a local anaesthetic?' He dismissed this possibility, saying that he had made only a limited investigation, and moved on to hope that cocaine would prove to be highly beneficial to the Peruvian economy, as it was extracted from the coca leaf, very much a home-grown product.

In 1870 in France, Charles Gazeau took up to 30 grammes of coca leaves and found that his appetite was completely suppressed; he thought this could be important for soldiers on a campaign. Military interest in the drug was not high, but in one minor yet interesting experiment in a newly united and aggressively minded Germany a decade later, Aschenbrandt clandestinely put cocaine into the water drunk by Bavarian soldiers on manoeuvres. He noticed that they became much more alert and considerably more plucky afterwards. There is no evidence, though, that the German high command was ever interested, no doubt believing more in the traditional values of training and discipline. In 1876, however, coca was recommended for use in both army and industry in the French *Dictionnaire encyclopédique des sciences médicales*.

Early in the 1870s, a Dr Charles Fauvel in Paris began to use cocaine in various throat medicines to relieve pain and assist in examining vocal chords. He got the drug from his cousin Angelo Mariani, now well on the way to making a fortune from his celebrated wine. Other doctors copied Fauvel's methods, but still a general connection between the drug and local anaesthesia was not made. Incidentally, Mariani worked almost exclusively with coca leaves, about which he probably knew more than any man or woman living. A sharp parting of the ways was soon to emerge, though, for while coca and its use was to remain well within the bounds of reasonable – and even demonstrably – good health, cocaine was to chart an altogether more stormy route. The course would be first set by the good Dr Sigmund Freud and recklessly followed by largely American interests, from the benign to the plainly bizarre. The phrase 'quick fix' leaps to mind, and for that bustling society, in too much of a hurry for its own good, cocaine had near-perfect credentials as the drug to take along for the ride.

In Britain, the coca leaf was by the 1870s an object of serious interest. In the *British Medical Journal* of April 1874, Dr Alexander Bennett discussed the physiological action of coca leaves. Following a long tradition, he took the leaves himself (as a healthy individual) and made notes. 'I was not able to convince myself that the drug thus administered had any special effects, with the exception of a sensation of slight local tingling of the tongue and mouth when the leaves were masticated for any length of time,' he wrote. He thought that the lack of effect might be due to the age of the leaf, or a failure by him to appreciate and apply the proper method of chewing. It is certainly true that although coca leaves which had been properly transported were available, storage conditions were frequently very poor, with the leaves left to deteriorate in sacks at the back of warehouses.

As a result of these inconclusive results, Dr Bennett sought to obtain a sample of cocaine ('the neutral principle of the leaf' as he put it) and 'after great difficulty' succeeded. He then experimented on animals to see if he could reach any further conclusions. Cocaine, he noted, was a stimulant, like *theine, caffeine, guaranine*, and *theobromine* (the active ingredient in chocolate). But unlike them he realised it was a powerful poison, terminating in death if enough was given to a subject. He thought all five chemicals identical in action and he added that, if used judiciously, all might find a use in medicine.

A little later, interest in the leaf was restimulated by the antics of the American endurance walker Edward Weston, who had appeared in Britain in 1876 to challenge local race-walking champions. Race walking, as with the bicycle fad shortly after, was one of many Victorian outdoor passions. Starting in Islington, north London, at the Royal Agricultural Halls, Weston undertook a 115-mile 24-hour trek. His British competitor dropped out after 14 hours, not looking at all well. Weston powered on and, observed a Mr Ashburton-Thompson at the time, as he later reported to the *British Medical Journal*:

> At intervals, as he persistently pursues his route, Weston may be seen to go through the actions of chewing; and a brown stain upon the lips, which the observant spectator may notice at the same time, leading to the suspicion that he is refreshing himself with a quid of tobacco. Yet it is well-known Weston renounces tobacco . . . on these occasions he is masticating a substance which, although credited with some of the properties of tobacco, is the most serviceable of its class for use under exertion. That substance is the dried leaf of the *Erythroxylon coca*.

Weston later asked Mr Ashburton-Thompson not to mention his use of the coca leaf; an early example, perhaps, of the use of stimulants in sporting events and a feeling among some that it is not quite 'cricket'. When Weston's use of coca got out, it caused the kind of row one might have expected. Yet ten years later, women runners in the USA were being aided by coca 'extract' and Vin Mariani (along with an increasing number of variations on the same theme) was seen to be essential to sports such as cycling.

On a less competitive note, the 78-year-old Dr Robert Christison of

Edinburgh reported that coca extract had helped him and a number of other elderly friends to walk long distances (up to 16 miles) without food or sleep, and had had no after-effects. As a result of this and other field 'experiments', the *British Medical Journal* once more proclaimed in an editorial that coca would turn out to be 'a new stimulant and a new narcotic [sic]: two forms of novelty in excitement which our modern civilisation is highly likely to esteem'. Within a month of this piece being published the journal was receiving inquiries from women who apparently hoped coca would give them strength and beauty 'for ever'. *The Lancet* had always taken a more barbed view of medical 'advances'. It countered in an issue dated the same as the *British Medical Journal*'s with a piece by Dr Dowdeswell, who, reviewing what was known rather than making any further experiment, concluded that the use of coca was more likely to be pernicious than not, and that all the anecdotal evidence from South America supported this opinion.

In the United States interest had begun to awaken to the curative powers of coca. In 1878, advertisements in the USA were recommending it for 'young persons afflicted with timidity in society' and as 'a powerful nervous excitant'. Also in 1878, Dr W.H. Bentley advocated coca as a cure for morphine addiction. It is important to note that Bentley – much criticised later for his views on this matter – was not suggesting that cocaine itself was the cure.

Up to that point cocaine, whilst clearly by far the stronger substance in its effects, had been the poor relative of the broad spectrum coca extract. The reason was simply one of supply and cost. One of the critical issues, still with us today, is the difference between the effects of the coca leaf taken as a whole and that of cocaine taken on its own. Bentley, writing in the early 1880s, could hardly have known that within a few years the use of cocaine would be substituted for use of coca in most of the literature on the subject. Writing in the *Detroit Therapeutic Gazette* he was cheerfully optimistic about coca, claiming to have used it himself for over ten years. Like many medical men of his time, he was faced with a still rising tide of disease, to be countered with very few medicines which worked. In an age when progress was seen to be an integral part of daily life, in which a burgeoning society was insisting on answers to everything, the embrace of the new would prove irresistible.

The idea of a miracle cure was not thought of as a myth in medicine a hundred years ago: it was an imperative. Bentley was by no means alone in thinking it might lie with the coca plant and its leaves. The liquid extract of coca was admitted to the *US Pharmacopoeia* in 1882. Two years before, an editorial in the *Louisville Medical News* proclaimed that 'one feels like trying coca, with or without the opium habit. A harmless remedy for the blues is imperial.' In Peru, meanwhile, another doctor, George Ward, doubted that coca had any more effect than tea or coffee – something borne out by modern research on coca leaf-chewing by Indians. Given these beliefs, the temptation to substitute the revved-up version, cocaine, precisely to get a faster hit, would be inevitable. All it required was what would amount to a marketing campaign.

If there is a single year in which cocaine may be said to have made its full mark on a first startled and then rapidly delighted world, it is 1884. It is a remarkable coincidence that almost exactly a hundred years later, crack cocaine burned itself indelibly into our lives and psyches, a nightmare compared with the halcyon dreams of an earlier age. But for twenty years, from 1884, cocaine – as well as coca – enjoyed, from both medical and popular opinion, an unbroken run of rave reviews. The man who, in a manner of speaking, gave us the first full performance, was a struggling Viennese medical student desperate to make his mark on an indifferent world.

In 1884 Sigmund Freud was locked into conventional medical studies. He was also desperately in love with his fiancée, Martha Bernays, who lived far away from the capital of Austro-Hungary, Vienna. His high level of sexual frustration over this state of affairs (he could see no quick way to make enough money to marry her) was largely responsible for causing him to suffer from a variety of neurotic symptoms. These he diagnosed himself as the same neurasthenia which apparently afflicted so many people. He constantly sought a way out of the dilemma thrown up by his own dangerous mixture of ambition and emotion.

Freud's solution, as related by himself, was 'to make a name for himself by discovering something important in either clinical or pathological medicine'. Into his life came cocaine, entering his consciousness through his avid reading of medical journals. The articles by Dr Bentley were of particular interest, since they dealt with the treatment by coca of morphine addiction and also of impotence. The impotence Freud knew all about; the addiction also, since one of his closest friends, Ernst von Fleischl-Marxow, had been addicted to morphine following the amputation of a thumb which had caused him appalling and constant 'phantom' pain.

In the spring of 1884, Freud bought a gramme of cocaine from Merck of

Darmstad. This was a huge investment for a penurious medical student: about a whole month's salary (in today's currency the gramme cost around 80p). Wasting no time once he obtained the precious crystals, he dissolved a twentieth in water and drank it. By his own account he was feeling tired. He later reported: 'a few minutes after taking cocaine, one experiences a sudden exhilaration and feeling of lightness'. To modern ears this sounds disingenuous as we know that cocaine's action is largely broken down in the stomach, but he was ingesting pharmaceutical pure cocaine, not a 'street' version and the mucous membrane in the throat would have absorbed some of the cocaine he took.

Freud hurried to his friend Fleischl-Marxow, who, according to a much-quoted passage, 'clutched at the new drug "like a drowning man"; within a few days he was taking it continuously'. Less than a year later Marxow was injecting up to a gramme a day. Later still he would begin to exhibit the signs of chronic cocaine abuse, including hallucinations in which he believed insects were crawling out of his skin. He died seven years after he first started to use the drug; Freud never forgave himself.

Freud's early enthusiasm for cocaine knew no bounds. Within a few months of his first purchase he was freely using it himself and giving it to friends and colleagues, as well as to his sister. He also sent some to Martha Bernays, probably in the hope that it would increase her sexual appetite to something like his own, which now, he believed, was fanned by his daily ingestion of the drug. He wrote:

> Woe to you, my Princess, when I come. I will kiss you quite red and feed you until you are plump. And if you wilfully resist, you shall see who is the stronger, a gentle little girl who doesn't eat enough or a big wild man with cocaine in his body.

It is clear from Freud's own writings that he used drugs as a substitute for sex and that they allowed his feelings towards Martha Bernays to become more easily expressed. More intriguing still, a recent paper by Jurgen von Scheidt in a German psychoanalytical journal has suggested that Freud's use of cocaine may have helped him to develop his own self-analysis and thus contributed to his *Weltanshauung*.

He had already published the first of four scientific papers on cocaine (*Über Coca*) in July 1884. According to his biographer Ernest Jones, it was the most complete paper on cocaine yet to appear. In it, he gave a detailed history of the coca plant and its use, an examination of the effects of cocaine on himself and provided a section on its potential uses: as a stimulant for depressives; to treat digestive disorders; to treat morphine and alcohol addiction; to treat asthma; as an aphrodisiac; and as a local anaesthetic. Jones also relates that this scientific paper contained 'a remarkable combination of objectivity and personal warmth, as though he [Freud] were in love with the object itself'. Looked upon from the distance of a hundred years, the 'science' shades into the distance and the 'love affair' is all too apparent. Freud, at this point, was not investigating cocaine by any means other than subjective observation, along with a highly selective review of the literature.

The issue of whether Freud became addicted to cocaine, in whatever sense we mean and even if only for a short time, is no longer open to much doubt. More intriguing is the question of how far it influenced his entire canon of thought. At least one author has suggested, reading between the lines of both Ernest Jones's biography and Freud's own writings, that far from stopping his use of cocaine in 1890, as both claim was the case, Freud almost certainly took it up again in 1892 and from this time on was snorting it, not injecting it. Further, Freud's thesis about the id (the unconscious) may well have developed out of his use of cocaine and led on to one of his seminal works, *The Interpretations of Dreams*, published in 1900. In that work there are a number of dreams which relate to syringes and to the nose.

The same train of thought also suggests that Freud's theories about sexuality may well have derived from his early experiences with cocaine (which frequently begin among users with what amounts to priapism, but rapidly lead to impotence allied with a paradoxically overheated *desire* for sex). It is also significant that Freud spent a lifetime after these early years eschewing any pain relief, in part brought on by remorse over Fleischl-Marxow. Possibly, though, this was the result of his much longer experience with cocaine and a continuing fear over his acknowledged addictive personality (manifest in his desire for cigars, a desire which would eventually kill him through cancer).

Given all these circumstances, it is perhaps unsurprising that Freud, too, missed the significance of his own last point in *Über Coca* about cocaine's anaesthetising effect, even though he specifically indicated that it was on the mucous membranes that cocaine acted most effectively. Instead of making his name as the discoverer of a local anaesthetic, however limited, he was shortly to be vilified as the author of the third scourge of humankind after alcohol and morphine.

It was to be Carl Kohler, another of his friends to whom he had casually given cocaine, who realised that the drug he had been seeking for years was literally in his pocket. A hiatus in the close-knit medical community at first suggested that this vital discovery would be credited to Leopold Koenigstein, who had also had the benefit of Freud's largesse in the matter of cocaine. But Koenigstein was obsessed with its vasoconstricting powers and told Kohler it was no use as an anaesthetic.

The eventual outcome – Kohler was credited with the discovery – came only after Koenigstein belatedly tried to snatch the prize from Kohler, publishing a simultaneous paper on cocaine and local anaesthesia. It was Freud who later insisted that Koenigstein retract his claim, which he did in a letter to a medical journal. It is also significant that Kohler never recognised, publicly or privately, that Freud ever had the slightest input into his researches. The truth is that Freud had asked Kohler to help him in *his* researches with cocaine. Freud's own explanation for why he failed to see this use of cocaine was, intriguingly, that he was distracted by a rare visit to his fiancée in the summer of 1884, no doubt carrying the remnants of his cocaine with him and hoping that Martha would succumb to his ardour.

When Kohler first experimented with cocaine he washed the cornea of the eye of a frog with it, and then pricked its eye and observed no response. Later he experimented on himself in the same way. Finally, on 15 September 1884, at the Heidelberg Ophthalmological Society, he gave a public demonstration. The results were as expected and cocaine's use as an anaesthetic was rapidly established. It was, however, to remain a relatively dangerous chemical to use in this way; many were to die until the invention of novocaine fifteen years later. Novocaine is a derivative without the unpredictability of cocaine on the central nervous system.

The moment of discovery was timely. The other generally available tools for the job were even cruder: ether or chloroform. But it is still worth wondering why it all took so long. The first known paper on coca's deadening power was read in 1857 in New York; in 1880 Coupart and Bordereau had described its use on the cornea of animal eyes. But for whatever reason, it was Kohler who got the acclamation and, within a few weeks of his paper's publication in Heidelberg, cocaine was being used in surgery for rhinology, laryngology, gynaecology, urology and, of course, dentistry.

After Kohler's insight, a spate of other anaesthetic uses of cocaine were employed. In the United States William Halstead, at John Hopkins University, discovered nerve blocking – also in 1884, and as a result of learning about Kohler's work – by injecting cocaine into nerve trunks. In 1892 Schleich brought in subcutaneous injection methods; in 1898 August Bier introduced spinal anaesthesia. In general, as with Freud, medical opinion was at first uncritically taken with this new-found wonder. Corning, who had discovered regional anaesthesia, is typical of the general mood: 'Of all the tonic preparations ever introduced to the notice of the professions, this is undoubtedly the most potent for good in the treatment of exhaustive and irritative conditions of the central nervous system.'

Cocaine, within this extremely short period of time, was well on the way to being accepted as the cure-all that medicine had long been seeking. Between July and December 1885 there were 27 articles, notes and letters on cocaine in the *New York Medical Journal*. In the same year the pharmaceutical company, Parke-Davis, brought out its hundred-page pamphlet, *Coca Erythroxylon and its Derivatives*. By then the American Hay Fever Association had adopted it as the remedy of choice; it was also being heavily promoted as a cure for colds and catarrh. William Hammond, a former surgeon-general in the US Army, suggested pure cocaine for use in inflammations of the mucous membrane and for preventing women from masturbating through the anaesthetising of the clitoris.

The use of cocaine in many of these cases was a reflection of the widely held view that it was useful in the treatment of a range of mental illnesses. Of these, neurasthenia was the most important. Today we might look upon this as a syndrome, much in the same category as ME or even 'sick building syndrome'. In a world where psychiatry was struggling with an increasing number of mentally ill people, with few diagnoses and fewer means of effective treatment, the happy coincidence of cocaine appeared nothing less than a miracle. And the world was beginning to believe once more, through the progress of science rather than religion, in miracles.

Patients with neurasthenia exhibited a dazzling array of sometimes contradictory symptoms: nervous dyspepsia, headaches, sleeplessness, hysteria, allergies (of which hay fever was commonplace), drunkenness, even epilepsy. The cause was increasingly attributed to the rate of change in American society, the same progress which was the rationale for its existence.

Cocaine, it was thought, could 'repair' the damaged and debilitated nerves created by an overheated society. Some doctors even believed it might improve mental ability; reports were coming in from all over the place (almost invariably from doctors) that its use stimulated the tired into activity, the exhausted into labour, the puzzled into the light of knowledge. The use of coca had by now been credited, discredited and credited again. If coca contained only a small percentage of cocaine, what could not the alkaloid itself do?

The pharmaceutical companies themselves were more than happy to rely on the positive evidence to help promote what was rapidly becoming a key product, whilst ignoring the slow but damning accretion of its addictive and dangerous physiological effects. Parke-Davis led the charge. It had been Parke-Davis's initiative which got Freud to endorse its own cocaine over that of Merck; a favour for which he was paid. Finally, in 1901 the American doctor, W. Golden Mortimer published his classic on coca and cocaine, *Peru: History of Coca*, in which he sums up all the favourable views on the leaf and the drug. Mortimer approved of the use of both leaf and crystal to aid French bicyclists as well as a championship lacrosse team.

The harsher pleasures of cocaine had been well documented by yet another doctor, this time a literary one. Conan Doyle's most noted creation, Sherlock Holmes, was a heavy user of injected cocaine. Holmes is first found using it in *A Scandal in Bohemia*, published in 1886, where Conan Doyle had him 'alternating week to week between cocaine and ambition'. It is probable that Conan Doyle had not imbibed the drug himself (or injected: he was a doctor). His description of the effects of cocaine suggest that he was confusing morphine with cocaine; 'the drowsiness of the drug' is how he puts it.

In 1888, with the *Sign of the Four*, Conan Doyle appears to have been alerted to cocaine's actual effect – so much so that we might surmise it was now based on personal knowledge. Holmes was injecting it three times a day and by 1891, in *The Final Problem*, he was exhibiting paranoid delusions, a classic symptom of acute abuse. It has been suggested that Professor Moriarty was a delusion of Holme's deranged mind and not real. Watson, proclaiming he has never heard of the man, is confronted by Holmes: 'Ay, there's the genius of the whole thing!' he cried. 'The man pervades London and no one has heard of him. That's what puts him on the pinnacle in the records of crime . . .'

Three years after Holmes disappears at the Reichenback Falls he is back (popular demand forced Conan Doyle to write more tales). However, this time he no longer uses cocaine and he no longer has much to say about Moriarty either. At least one modern book and film has developed the idea of Holmes's underlying problem. In *The Seven Per Cent Solution* which, given the history of cocaine, rather neatly has Holmes being analysed in Vienna by Freud, Holmes's Moriarty delusion is shown, by hypnosis, to have been a memory of his old maths teacher. In the film Freud first gets Holmes to stop using cocaine, another neat twist.

Whatever the merits of the Sherlock Holmes case, what evidence is there to suggest that Robert Louis Stevenson's *Dr Jekyll and Mr Hyde* was written under a rather more benign use of the same drug? The most compelling argument is that Stevenson, who wrote the book in 1885, managed to complete the book twice – he burned the first draft after his wife commented unfavourably on it – in just six days. He was acutely sick with tuberculosis at this time, but was apparently able to write 120,000 words in longhand in under a week. Further, all this took place in 1885, the year when cocaine's miraculous healing powers for all and sundry were being heavily advertised in medical journals throughout the western world. Stevenson's wife had been avidly reading these in the hope of finding anything to help him. She said after his death: 'The amount of work this involved was appalling; that an invalid in my husband's condition of health should have been able to perform the manual labour seems incredible.' Indeed.

As well, Stevenson had previously been taking morphine, not a drug known to improve the rate at which anything coherent could be written. Later, his stepson said: 'The mere physical feat was tremendous; and instead of harming him, it [cocaine] roused and cheered him inexpressibly.' Some writers on this issue have gone further, suggesting that the potion Dr Jekyll takes is itself cocaine; this seems less likely. But although cocaine had had its *annus mirabilis*, its first impresario was beginning to lower the curtain on his unpredictable protégé.

Freud began to pull back from some of the first euphoric conclusions contained in *Über Coca* in a further paper written in July 1887. This one was soberly entitled *Craving for and Fear of Cocaine* and he acknowledged that the drug ought not to be used for morphine addiction (Fleischl-Marxow was still alive at this time, but slipping slowly into oblivion). Freud still insisted, 'all reports of addiction to cocaine and deterioration from it refer to morphine addicts . . . *Cocaine has claimed no other, no victims on its own*' [Freud's italics].

Freud did not know at this time that the inventor of the nerve-block use of cocaine, William Halstead, was falling more and more under its spell. Halstead had independently published four papers on cocaine between 1884 and 1885 and he was, like Freud, captivated by the possibilities. Thirty years on, in 1918, he admitted what a toll the drug had taken on his own life and suggested that at least three of his assistants had died from over-using it.

The Halstead case is important. Within a week of hearing of the Kohler experiments William Halstead, then a young surgeon and chief of the New York Roosevelt Hospital outpatient department, began to self-administer cocaine. He was joined in this by his friends and associates, Richard Hall and Frank Hartley. They extended their experiments to include students at the hospital – and patients. Within a year the Halstead team had used nerve-blocks on 1,000 patients.

In 1885 Halstead came to Europe; his visit included Vienna. He became addicted to cocaine to such an extent that one of his friends, William Welch, chartered a schooner with a crew of three to take Halstead on a voyage around the Caribbean in an effort to break his habit. This attempt failed. A second attempt, using the conventional method of checking him into a hospital, took away Halstead's craving for cocaine but shifted it onto morphine. Halstead claimed to be cured of that addiction by 1887 and he went on to become the first professor of surgery at John Hopkins School of Medicine, where he spent the rest of his life. After his death, it was revealed he had never, in fact, been cured of his morphine addiction.

The issue of abuse and misuse, as well as that of addiction, continues to afflict the debate about cocaine right up to the present day. As late as 1989 an American medical journal published a research paper which refuted the idea that cocaine was addictive, that it could merely, like anything else, be abused. Cocaine did produce in many of the early (heavy and long-term) users a level of need which led to their downfall. This is quite separate from cocaine's other, and soon to emerge, contemporary negative associations – principally with prostitution, crime and, most important for the time in which the reaction set in, with 'crazed niggers', as more than one newspaper report described.

Cocaine burst out of its medical ghetto after the euphoria of the medics gave notice to a wider public of the new wonder. Nearly the entire story of cocaine's legal use by the general public is contained in the United States. By the 1890s cocaine, as well as coca, could be bought at any downtown

American pharmacy, in a wide variety of forms. The USA was obsessed with patent medicine in an age where, once the east coast had been left behind, genuine doctors were very few and far between. Americans, too, in the spirit of their age, believed fervently in self-help and in progress with a capital P. Cocaine, with its uplifting and euphoric effects well documented, fitted perfectly with the notion that a panacea existed and, fortuitously, had arrived in time to save the day. This was the era of Boosterism and cocaine could hardly have fitted the bill better.

By 1890 it was being sold in pharmacies as a cure for alcoholism, asthma, the common cold, whooping cough, dysentery, haemorrhoids, neuralgia, seasickness, vomiting in pregnancy, sore nipples, vaginismus, gonorrhoea and syphilis, as well, as we have seen, for morphine and opium addiction. Notoriously, one of these patent medicines, Ryno's Hay Fever-'n'-Catarrh Remedy, was 99.95 per cent pure cocaine. Everybody was being swept up with the idea that cocaine had the answers to many ailments. The *New York Times* in 1885 proclaimed: 'The new uses to which cocaine has been applied with success in New York include hay fever, catarrh, and toothache, and it is now being experimented with in cases of seasickness. Cocaine will cure the worst cold in the head ever heard of.'

During the 1890s in the United States, it was possible to saunter into a pharmacy and buy cocaine to sniff, to nibble, to suck, to smoke (in cigarettes), to rub in as ointment, to gargle and to insert as a suppository. Down the road you might drink Metcalf's Coca Wine. An advertisement for this concoction showed the coca leaf at the centre with a short history of its use in South America. It then listed ailments which could be cured if the wine were taken three times a day. Among other things, it claimed to have the power to cure impotency: 'Elderly people have found it a reliable aphrodisiac superior to any other drink.' As well this, 'Athletes, pedestrians and baseball players have found by practical experience that a steady course of coca taken both before and after any trial of strength or endurance will impart energy to every movement, and prevent fatigue.'

It was inevitable, given the extraordinary success of Angelo Mariani's Vin Mariani, that sooner or later he would be faced with competition. Given the United States' love-hate affair with the whisky bottle so beloved of the old West and the whiff of prohibition on the wind, it was also likely that any imitator in America would eventually devise a tonic which kept in the coca but left out the booze.

It was in this feverish atmosphere that the original formulas of coca extract in soft drinks were invented. The truly original Coca-Cola we know today was based, unoriginally, on Vin Mariani, with the alcohol taken out. This drink was to emerge triumphant out of the many attempts to define and refine the coca tonic drink, on a scale still hard to grasp. Coca-Cola was a phenomenon almost from the start. Far from being a mere drink, it rapidly moved on to help define the way that the rest of the world viewed the USA and its place in the twentieth century. At home in the States, though, long after the cocaine was taken out of the coca extract (its core ingredient), it was usually ordered in bars and drug stores as 'a shot in the arm'.

The history of Coca-Cola really began decades before the drink was first conceived of, thousands of miles away, as we have already glimpsed. It began with the man who not only gave the western world its first proper taste of the 'divine plant', but who was to be heavily imitated by the Coca-Cola Company in his fervent, not to say obsessive, marketing methods.

The toast, ladies and gentlemen, is to Angelo Mariani and his remarkable tonic wine!

PART TWO

EXCORIATION AND EXORCISM

4

FEVER!

WITH THE HINDSIGHT OF 140 YEARS, it is difficult to overestimate the importance of Angelo Mariani to both the story of coca and the entire modern soft drinks industry, notably Coca-Cola. To a chaotic and unregulated marketplace, Mariani was to bring first a product which people could genuinely believe in and second, a huge marketing exercise which ensured its lasting success. Third, he would introduce a drink which was, in every respect, 'the real thing'.

Angelo Mariani was born in Batia, the largest town in Corsica, and raised in a family of chemists and doctors. Around the time of Albert Niemann's experiments leading to the isolation of cocaine, he moved to Paris. There, intrigued by the tales he was hearing about this magic plant from South America, Mariani acquired some coca leaves for himself; just how remains unclear. After his own less-than-scientific experiments in chewing the leaves, he was convinced that they worked. But still he held back, not immediately plunging into devising a means by which they might be introduced to a Europe increasingly hungry for new experiences. He read travellers' tales, seeking out those where the use of coca leaves by the Indians was mentioned.

Mariani noted a crucial detail: the Indians frequently rejected the more bitter leaves, even though they had the higher cocaine content. He studied what was known about the varieties of coca leaf and acquired a lasting knowledge of the often subtle aromatic qualities of different kinds, picked in different places and at different times. In short, he studied the coca leaf much as others had studied the tea leaf.

At the same time, he was aware that *chewing* coca leaves was looked upon by European tastes in much the same way as tobacco chewing – not to be done in polite society. Instead, Mariani blended those coca leaves he thought best suited to his purpose and steeped them in good Bordeaux wine. The result was Vin Mariani and he set about marketing it as a tonic wine and stimulant for the tired brain. He was also careful to get endorsements from doctors. The year in which he launched this new beverage was 1863.

In a fairly short time, he became the world's biggest importer of coca leaf and Mariani was on the way to making his fortune. Later, there would be lozenges to suck, elixirs and tea to drink and pâté to eat. The majority were made from the coca leaf – Mariani rarely used pure cocaine. Later still, advertisements for the wine would say, *inter alia*:

> We cannot aim to gain support for our preparation through cheapness; we give a uniform, effective and honest article, and respectfully ask personal testing of Vin Mariani strictly on its own merits . . . Inferior so-called Coca preparations (variable solutions of Cocaine and cheap wines), which have been proved worthless, even harmful, in effect, bring into discredit and destroy confidence in a valuable drug.

In 1901, when W. Golden Mortimer wrote his classic book *On Coca*, he dedicated it to Mariani, calling him 'a recognised exponent of the "Divine Plant", the first to render coca to the world'. By this time Mariani himself had collected most of what would eventually become a thirteen-volume set of encomia on his wine from the world of the great and the good. This massive set of books is now a bibliophile collector's item. The Queen is reputed to have a set, passed down through the family.

Mariani, who knew a good thing when he saw or heard about it, wrote numerous articles as well as books about his beloved coca. The most significant of his books is *Coca and its Therapeutic Applications* (1890). In the introduction to this book Mariani says:

> Each race has its fashions and fancies. The Indian munches the betel; the Chinaman woos with passion the brutalising intoxication of opium; the European occupies his idle hours or employs his leisure ones in smoking, chewing or snuffing tobacco. *Guided by a happier instinct, the native of South America has adopted Coca* [my emphasis]. When young he robs his father of it; later on, he devotes his first savings to its purchase. Without it he would fear vertigo on the summit of the Andes, and weaken at his severe labour in the mines. It is with

him everywhere; even in his sleep he keeps his precious quid in his mouth.

He goes on a little later to add, 'the aim of this modest work is to offer to the medical profession a short account of the history of Coca, and of the investigations which it has called forth up to the present day'. The book is a model of understated but carefully produced data. Beginning with the 'botanical character of *Crythroxylon coca*', it continues with its cultivation and harvesting and moves on to the history of the plant. Mariani then attempts to deal with what was known about its physiological effects, mentioning the siege of La Paz [the capital of modern Bolivia] in 1781, where it had been reported that only those inhabitants who chewed coca were able to endure the hunger and fatigue which had resulted.

Mariani goes on to quote only favourable reports about the leaf, adding that coca was seen as an aphrodisiac. 'The fact that the Peruvian Venus was represented as holding in her hand a leaf of Coca was suggested as a proof in support of this opinion,' he says. 'Dr Unanue speaks of "certain *coqueros*, eighty years of age and over, and yet capable of such prowess as young men in their prime would be proud of".'

He goes on to deal with cocaine in fairly short order, mentioning its chemistry and the use of it by Kohler before returning to the coca leaf. Mariani suggests that coca is useful for diseases of the mouth, for example in ulcers or where the gums are bleeding and for diseases of the throat, pharynx and larynx. He quotes Charles Fauvel, his cousin, as his source. For diseases of the stomach, he suggests that coca may be useful for any number of complaints. Finally, he writes that where a disease has 'a depressing action on the nervous system . . . the effect of Coca is truly marvellous' and quotes Gubler in *Commentaires de Thérapeutique*: 'Coca, very much like tea and coffee, lends to the nervous system the force with which it is charged.'

The last chapter is devoted, inevitably, to the Mariani range of products. He modestly reports:

> Under the esteemed patronage of our greatest medical celebrities, our preparations are known all over the world; they have reached all classes of society and everywhere, in the largest cities as well as in the small villages, men, women and children, in fact, convalescents of all ages now know the name of the salutary plant, which it has been our effort

to popularise, though strictly according to the code of medical ethics and by those channels approved of by the entire medical profession [Mariani claimed direct endorsements from over 7,000 doctors].

Mariani was by now the world expert on coca, as well as knowing a lot about cocaine. He also provided Mortimer with samples of coca grown in his own conservatories. Mortimer considered the Mariani preparations superior to every other in both flavour and efficacy.

In an age when advertising was becoming recognisably modern, Mariani was among those who saw its power. He also realised the importance of what we would now call celebrity endorsement and the need to get and keep on board those professionals at whom his product was initially aimed. He kept up a relentless pressure the late twentieth century would understand only too well, believing that you can never over-sell something if you believe in it. Mariani radiated his belief, both in his growing range of coca-based products and in the coca plant and its wonderful leaf. As the years went by, he solicited more and more letters from all over the world. Among the thousands and thousands of these letters, here is a very small sample, to give a flavour both of who wrote back and the level of praise for Vin Mariani and its effects.

Alexander Dumas: 'Mariani, your sweet flasks delight my mouth.'

Thomas Edison: 'Monsieur Mariani, I take pleasure in sending you one of my photographs for publication in your album, yours very truly.'

Anatole France: 'It is true that Mariani coca wine spreads a subtle fire through the organism.'

The Lumière Brothers: 'To our friend Mariani, whose wine gives us strength.'

President William McKinley: 'My dear sir, Please accept thanks on the President's behalf and on my own for your courtesy in sending a case of the celebrated Vin Mariani, with whose tonic virtues I am already acquainted, and will be happy to avail myself of in the future as occasion may require.' (John Addison Porter, Secretary to the President)

Oscar II (king of Sweden and Norway): 'My hearty thanks.'

Jules Verne: 'Since a single bottle of Mariani's extraordinary coca wine guarantees a lifetime of a hundred years, I shall be obliged to live until the year 2700. Well, I have no objections! Yours very gratefully.'

Cardinal Lavigerie: 'Your coca from America gave my European priests the strength to civilise Asia and Africa.'

Jules Massenet: 'To my friend Angelo Mariani, in grateful memory of the land of coca.'

Pope Leo XIII sent Mariani a gold medal in the care of a Cardinal and this letter: 'His Holiness has deigned to commission me to thank the distinguished donor in His holy name, and to demonstrate His gratitude in a material way as well. His Holiness does me the honour of presenting M. Mariani with a gold medal containing His venerable coat-of-arms.'

Pope Pius X: 'His Holiness has received the bottles of coca wine [which] has been really welcomed and asks that his pleasure be known to yourself.'

The Csars of Russia, the British Prince of Wales (later Edward VII), Zola, Ibsen and General Ulysses Grant also gave testimony to the healing and restorative powers of the wine. Grant, who took a teaspoon of the wine a day in the last five months of his life, may not have finished his memoirs without it. Ten years into the twentieth century, Louis Bleriot wrote: 'I took the precaution of bringing a small flask of Mariani wine along with me, and it was a great help. Its energetic action sustained me during the crossing of the Channel.'

Mariani's reputation did not, however, live on as much as one might suppose. In 1970 a half bottle of his original wine, dated 1880, sold for a mere four pounds at a London auction (about £40 at today's prices).

It has long been a wonder why, knowing there was very little cocaine in the leaves that Mariani used, so many drinkers of the beverage went overboard in their praise of its effect on them. Only in the last decade have researchers discovered that cocaine and alcohol combine in the liver to form a compound, cocaethylene, about which little is still known except that it may well potentiate the effect of both. If so, it would certainly go some way towards explaining why the praises heaped on Mariani's principal product were so high. Mariani recommended three glasses a day, each of six fluid ounces. A chemist in 1886 found 0.12 grains of cocaine per fluid ounce of the wine. Over a day, if one followed Mariani's advice, this would mean ingesting 2.16 grains (about two to three good lines of averagely cut cocaine). This would have given a more than adequate kick, especially in conjunction with the Bordeaux base and considering current knowledge of cocaethylene.

The wine, he explained in *Coca and its Therapeutic Applications*, used three sources for his coca which, in thirty years, had never produced a case of cocainism (at this time just beginning to be recognised as a potentially serious problem). The elixir, also produced by his company, was more alcoholic, 'very agreeable to the taste, and three times as highly charged with the aromatic principles of the Coca leaf as the Vin Mariani; therefore,' he added, 'it should be taken in doses of a liqueur glassful, in the morning upon rising, and after the two principal meals.' If Mariani truly meant that the elixir contained three times the amount of coca leaf, then three glasses of this would have provided quite a kick to the user. He quoted a Dr Collins as saying that the liqueur acts 'heroically in anaemia, chlorosis and rickets'.

While Vin Mariani did not contain cocaine, the Mariani pastilles did. To be used in the same way as the pâté (for coughs, catarrh and stomach complaints), the pastilles had two milligrammes of cocaine hydrochloride added. They were recommended for, among other complaints, smokers' coughs. The tea Mariani produced was useful for travellers to remote locations, and to mountain climbers, where coca was put back to the use for which, at least in part, it had originally been used.

By now a millionaire, Mariani was on a roll and he knew it. He was bringing a revolution in marketing and sales techniques to Europe and the rest of the world. Part of his key strategy was to sell through the medical establishment. The value of Vin Mariani was that it worked in an age where much was fake, much was only partially successful, and some was liable to be both fake and lethal to the user. These lessons – create a product, ensure its purity and sell on – were to be well learned by a soft-drink inventor in Atlanta.

But while there were those who saw that the future lay in selling tonics and patent medicines the public could rely upon, many others were happy to peddle what they could get away with. In this they were amply assisted by the same public which, by the middle of the nineteenth century, had cheerfully come to embrace a huge range of newfangled theories about illness and health. This attitude was reinforced by the state of conventional medicine, which had hardly progressed in hundreds of years. Although we now live in an entirely different medical world, today's interest in and embracing of a range of holistic medical practices suggests that what goes around, comes around.

Self-medication among both rich and poor, along with a degree of faddishness in medical matters, was by no means new a century and a half ago. Until the nineteenth century it had generally meant going outdoors to seek well-accredited herbs and other plants, used for a huge range of ailments. There were books to aid the learned, the majority of which either explicitly or implicitly attacked the medical orthodoxy of the day. Herbalism was added to in the nineteenth century by other new theories of good health and methods of treatment: homoeopathy, hydropathy and mesmerism among them. The slow decline of herbalism during this time was due to the huge shift in the population away from the countryside, where traditions of self-help were aided by proximity to possible cures, to industrial towns and cities where a raft of new, often deadly diseases floated on a tide of filth.

In this changing world, one drug left a permanent mark: opium and, from 1803, its far more potent derivative, morphine, named for the god of sleep. Morphine became a drug which would creep into the lives of many professional and other middle-class people; morphine kits, with syringes for self-administration, were sold over the counter from the middle of the century. Inappropriate use of morphine was to emerge as one of the great medical and social scourges of the age.

Opium had been known about for a very long time in the east. In Britain, opium had been used since the seventeenth century when it had been highly praised by Dr Thomas Sydenham. It was not until well into the 1840s, though, that it became widely used in medicine; the reasons why are intriguing. Opium was available to the man or woman in the street through prescribing chemists; invariably it was 'eaten' or, more usually, drunk as laudanum, or tincture of opium, although it could be bought as powder or pill.

The use of opium by the Romantic poet Samuel Coleridge and others is widely known. But it was through the writings of Thomas de Quincey that many more Victorians came to know of the strengths and weaknesses of the drug. De Quincey had started using laudanum to help a chronic stomach condition and progressed to using opium in ever-increasing amounts. In *Confessions of an English Opium Eater*, his experience of this is chronicled in great detail. The book, first published as a series of articles in 1821, remains a classic text, detailing the highs and lows of addiction. For contemporary readers it would by no means have acted as a deterrent. De Quincey eventually managed to reduce his daily intake, but he remained a heavy user of opium until his death, aged 74, in 1859.

This is de Quincey on his first encounter with the drug which was to change his life:

> Opium! Dread agent of unimaginable pleasure and pain! I had heard of it as I had of manna or of ambrosia, but no further: how unmeaning a sound was it at that time! What solemn chords does it now strike upon my heart! What heart-quaking vibrations of sad and happy remembrances! . . . It was a Sunday afternoon, wet and cheerless; a duller spectacle this earth of ours has not to show than a rainy Sunday in London. My road homewards lay through Oxford Street; and near the stately pantheon (as Mr Wordsworth has obligingly called it) I saw a druggist's shop. The druggist, unconscious minister of celestial pleasures! – as if in sympathy with the rainy Sunday, looked dull and stupid, just as any mortal druggist might be expected to look on a Sunday: and when I asked for the tincture of opium, he gave it to me as any other man might do: and furthermore, out of my shilling, returned to me what seemed to be real copper halfpence, taken out of a real wooden drawer. Nevertheless, in spite of such indications of humanity, he has ever since existed in my mind as the beatific vision of an immortal druggist, sent down to earth on a special mission to myself.

It was, as de Quincey explains, a fateful meeting. At home he took the quantity prescribed:

> In an hour, oh! heavens! What a revulsion! What an upheaving, from its lowest depths, of the inner spirit! What an apocalypse of the world within me! That my pains vanished, was now a trifle in my eyes – this negative effect was swallowed up in the immensity of those positive effects which had opened before me – in the abyss of divine enjoyment thus suddenly revealed. Here was a panacea for all human woes: here was the secret of happiness, about which philosophers had disputed for so many ages, at once discovered: happiness might now be bought for a penny, and carried in the waistcoat pocket, portable ecstasies might be had corked up in a pint bottle: and peace of mind could be sent down in gallons by the mail coach.

Access to opium through chemists or druggists was to be a bugbear to doctors throughout the century. They failed to check its widespread use, although chemists were regulated from 1868 by the Pharmacy Act.

Conventional medicine was going through its own crisis. The decisive issue was the degree to which patients were rejecting so-called 'heroic' treatments, which went back to the Middle Ages – procedures like bleeding, cupping and purging. Set against these treatments, laudanum must have been balm indeed. The drug was also pushed by former East India Company medics who had used it during various epidemics in India. Opium mixed with calomel was one of the most frequently used potions in the various cholera outbreaks in Victorian Britain.

More generally, laudanum was used for cases of diarrhoea, stomach ailments, headaches, general pain relief and, frequently, to quieten children. Its ubiquity during the nineteenth century is not in doubt. Queen Victoria took it, as she also took cannabis, for the relief of severe period pains. The humblest of her subjects took it, too; tincture of opium had the added advantage of being extremely cheap. So, from the 1840s, opium/laudanum became the drug of choice for both doctors and their patients. By 1880 a huge range of patent medicines contained opium and even the cures for 'opiomania', of the kind de Quincey would have known about, often contained opium. The growing availability of the syringe allowed morphine – opium's chemical heart – to be administered intravenously. Suddenly, the stakes were dramatically upped. As we have seen, cocaine came only a little later to play a significant part in its own downfall as the 'cure' for morphine addiction.

For most people, though, the question remained of how to stay in reasonably good health. When one considers that aspirin was not discovered until the 1890s, only a year or two before diacetyl-morphine (or heroin), this puts many of the events surrounding popular fears about ill health into context. The century was to witness a huge growth in over-the-counter medicines, the result of the scientific revolution which accompanied the industrial. Urbanisation was to play a part, continuing to force the pace of medical advance, but progress in all things was the catch-phrase of the age.

Nowhere was this more apparent than on the other side of the Atlantic. The post-Civil War period of reconstruction, from the 1870s on, saw the expansion of the United States into its own backyard – the West. This in turn led to a society which, while still taking Europe as its model for civilised behaviour and society manners, was increasingly determined to carve its own path, wherever that might lead. In short, it was an edgy, pushy society, in which individuals constantly sought excitement as well as certainty.

The growth of neurotic illnesses such as neurasthenia was as big a problem in the United States as it was in Europe, with the added difficulty that America suffered for a long time from an acute shortage of doctors. If Europeans lighted upon self-medication to save money and because much medicine was doubted, in the States it was often the only thing available. Throughout the last third of the last century an increasing number of patent medicines were available through the efforts of the American pharmaceutical companies. These were set against the quack remedies of 'snake oil' salesmen who peddled their wares at country fairs, and from door to door, ranch to ranch.

The pharmaceutical companies were, of course, also advertising to doctors – whence came the first praises for cocaine. Often isolated, probably not well trained, and still with little in their *materia medica* to help genuine cases, doctors were also in competition with a range of propriety medicines, tonics and pick-me-ups. In an age of self-reliance, when education and 'get-up-and-go' were twin aspirational goals, many of their patients were chafing against convention. The worship of the new and the novel was perhaps never so great.

And, as with Sigmund Freud in Europe, folk were constantly looking at ways of making both a fortune and a name.

Vin Mariani was no less popular in the United States than it was in Europe as the nerve tonic of choice for those who knew about and could afford it. Mariani's successes were not to go unchallenged in the New World. Despite his formidable operation, others took note and tried their luck. By the early 1890s, there were nineteen other coca wines on the market. The huge patent medicine market in the USA helped. One estimate suggests that by 1900 there were 25,000 patent medicines on the market. There were enormous fortunes to be made in patent medicines and, as many were not only false in their claims but entirely made up of undeclared ingredients, these medicines were often dangerous. It was the patent medicine industry which helped the rapid growth of the American newspaper business; up to half a newspaper might be filled with adverts making outrageous claims, in the main completely unchallenged. The market was explosive: the population of the USA grew from 50 million in 1880 to 91 million in 1910. There were 18 million new immigrants to be accommodated in all senses, each one a potential customer.

Into this overheated and overcrowded marketplace came a wide range of soft drinks (carbonated water had been invented in the 1870s). Of all the patented drinks of the time, it is Coca-Cola which is remembered best, although Dr Pepper was invented more or less at the same time. Early advertisements for the latter show a naked woman in the sea, her crotch covered by a wave with the slogan 'aids digestion and restores vim, vigour and vitality'. Coca-Cola was also pushed as an aid to digestion in early advertisements. In the early 1900s, its campaigns also featured seductive women apparently satisfied in more ways than one by a bottle of the drink. Much of this early history is now heavily glossed over by the Company, ever anxious in its marketing efforts and embarrassed about some of the more dubious methods by which the world's favourite drink was once advertised.

Coca-Cola was by no means the only coca-based product, nor the only one which early on combined coca leaves, kola nuts (a source of caffeine) and carbonated water. Its inventor, John Pemberton, was a Georgia-born doctor who had also trained as a pharmacist. Early on in his medical career, he had been seduced by the herbalist theories of Samuel Thompson and it was as a nerve tonic that Coca-Cola first made its mark. Its success was also tied to the huge impact that the soda fountain had on urban and suburban American life.

Pemberton opened a chemist's shop in Columbus, Ohio, in 1852, when he was just 21. In 1869 he made the decisive move in returning to Georgia, where he settled in Atlanta, then going through a post-Civil War boom. Pemberton read the Christison papers published in Britain about the properties of the coca leaf and, no doubt reinforced by what he read and saw elsewhere about Vin Mariani, produced his own French Coca wine. This, he announced, contained only Peruvian coca and also extract of African kola nuts, as well as *Damiana* plant extract. Pemberton, like Mariani, stressed the medical benefits of his drink, claiming that, as well as curing mental and physical exhaustion, it was 'a most wonderful invigorator of the sexual organs'.

Drug journals of the 1880s were full of recipes for coca wines; the majority were cheap imitations of Vin Mariani, using poor wines and simply adding cocaine. By 1885 the Mariani company was warning potential buyers of the dangers of the alternatives. Pemberton did not produce an inferior wine, since he based his version directly on that of his French rival. It was in his use of the kola nut – long known in the west coast of Africa as an aphrodisiac, as well as for providing extra energy – that Pemberton was to make perhaps the most significant change. Caffeine, contained in the kola nut, has in many respects become the legal version of cocaine; it is, like cocaine, an alkaloid with some of the same effects.

By the mid-1880s Pemberton's wine was selling well, but at this point it seemed as though Georgia would become a prohibition state. (It did, but only for a year between 1886 and 1887.) Pemberton was forced to reinvent his drink without alcohol: the result was Coca-Cola, more or less as it is known today. From 1902 or thereabouts, the cocaine content of the coca leaves was removed. The current line taken by the Coca-Cola Company is that Coca-Cola never had cocaine in it: there is a grain of truth in this, in so far as many of the cheaper imitations which tried their luck on the back of Coca-Cola's success simply added pure cocaine. But Coca-Cola did contain coca leaves in their entirety and Pemberton was well aware that this helped sell the drink. An early (1896) advertisement in the *National Druggist* ran this advertisement:

It seems to be a law of nature that the more valuable and efficacious a drug is, the nastier and more unpleasant its taste. It is therefore quite a triumph over nature that the Coca-Cola Co. of Atlanta, Ga., have achieved in their success in robbing coca leaves and the kola nut of the exceedingly nauseous and disagreeable taste while retaining their wonderful medicinal properties, and the power of restoring vitality and raising the spirits of the weary and debilitated.

Pemberton, who was a morphine addict and who might well have believed that coca, if not cocaine, was a cure for morphine addiction, was also a poor businessman, constantly in need of partners who would be able to help him out. His addiction could hardly have helped his business acumen. In 1886 he took on Frank Robinson who realised that in the market conditions then prevailing, he would have to take urgent and drastic measures to push Pemberton's new drink. What he did was to issue free samples to all and sundry. The local soda fountains filled with eager customers asking for 'the real thing'.

Coca-Cola originally came as a syrup, to be mixed in the elaborate soda fountains springing up all over America. The soda fountain phenomenon grew throughout the 1870s and 1880s. One contemporary writer called them 'temples resplendent in crystal marble and silver' and they had exotic names: Frost King; Snow-Drop; Aurora Borealis. The biggest could dispense 300 drink combinations and might have cost $40, 000. One key to success was to market soft drinks as exotic, as the soda fountain, in all its sparkling glory, implied; another was to emphasise their health-giving potential. Soda fountains remain a uniquely American invention. Mary Gay Humphries, writing in 1891 without reference to Coca-Cola, said: 'Soda water is an American drink. It is as essentially American as porter, Rhine wine, and claret are distinctively English, German, and French.' Competition between owners of the fountains was fierce.

Because Coca-Cola, along with most other beverages of the kind, came as syrup to be mixed, it was possible to ask for more than one 'shot' at a time. It seems fairly certain than many did, thereby upping their intake of all the ingredients, notably the cocaine and the caffeine. It is easy to appreciate the enthusiasm with which this coca-based and caffeine-containing drink was received.

Coca-Cola succeeded where others failed, not because it had some unique and magic formula but because it was aggressively advertised and marketed. Although Frank Robinson was the first to see the way ahead, it was with Asa Candler, who joined the nascent Company in 1891, that the story really began. Candler was to espouse a heady message which combined Coca-Cola with patriotism, religion and capitalism. It was to be his vision that created the legend and ensured that, despite a number of potentially crippling setbacks, this drink would be the one almost everyone would soon ask for.

Pemberton sold a share of the Company to Candler, but he was gaily selling more shares in his enterprise than he had; the total added to more than 100 per cent. It was hardly to matter. When the product began selling it had a decade of success, boosted, though by no means carried, by its heady mixture of contents. The question of whether the cocaine content – always a small portion of the bulked-up syrup – could have made all the difference is hardly relevant. Coca-Cola's formula may have been kept a secret for many years (although it is now published); the magic was in the mystique surrounding this cola drink. The lessons of Vin Mariani were well learned; but Vin Mariani would survive into the twentieth century only to fade away by the 1920s. Coca-Cola, by then without any cocaine, would go on to storm not just the United States but the rest of the world.

As its success became more and more apparent in the United States it was much imitated, as Vin Mariani had been: Cafe Cola, Kos-Kola, Kola-Ade, Celery-Cola, Koca-Nola, Wiseola, Rococola, Vani-Kola, Afri-Kola, even Koke, all came and went. Yet we can say this much: all were born on the wings of a boom for all that was fresh, modern and exotic. They all advertised themselves heavily as a drink which contained a known stimulant.

For Coca-Cola, rapidly becoming the soft drink the American public wanted above all others, one of the questions was how to make it both completely consistent in quality and readily transportable. Part of that availability was to come through bottling it on an industrial scale. The result of this was that anyone could go and buy it, not just the habitués of the soda fountains. And that meant that children – and blacks – could readily obtain and drink it. The greatest fears, which must be seen in the context of the year 1900, were not that children might get over-excited but that blacks, often compared to children in their abilities and level of understanding, most certainly would.

The demise of the cocaine content in Coca-Cola partly lay in this move towards bottling. It also lay in a growing understanding, by the turn of the century, that cocaine was definitely no longer the 'wonder drug' it had first been seen to be, even if that drug were locked into the coca leaf. As well, early on in the twentieth century, moves were afoot to get both state and federal legislation in place which would demand that manufacturers of foods and drinks clearly labelled all the ingredients they used. But first we have to turn to the moral panic which began to sweep America in the 1900s, a panic that was increasingly associated with still-legal drugs, with fears over rising crime and, specifically in relation to cocaine, with Southern blacks.

5

ALIEN NATION: THE USA, DRUGS AND RACE

THE CONTINUING SUCCESS OF COCA-COLA above all its rivals was due to a heady mixture of the right product at the right time, inspired marketing and massive relentless advertising. The success of this formula continues to the present day. Part of the marketing was based on convincing consumers that Coca-Cola represented part of keeping up with – and even being ahead of – the times. Quite early on, Coca-Cola began to be sold in factory-produced bottles, although the distinctive 'classic' bottle shape in which it is still sold today was not designed until 1911. It was, in one of those curious footnotes to history, based on the shape of a cacao seed, not the seed of the *Erythroxylon* plant, the artist apparently having mistaken coca and cacao in the local library.

Bottled soft drinks in the early 1900s were as modern as you could get and, as time passed, they became automatically associated with quality control and a uniform product. From the Company's point of view, it meant control over the contents in every sense. And, once bottled, the drink became much more widely available; no longer was it necessary to go to a local drug store with its soda fountain to buy it.

In the South, soda fountains were, by and large, out of bounds to blacks, through casually applied, but universally enforced, formal (legal) and informal segregation. Along with the rest of America, blacks began enthusiastically to embrace the all-American beverage: factory bottled Coca-Cola. But there is evidence that they were already discovering the altogether more powerful delights of cocaine itself from other sources. This came about in two ways. First, white employees were giving their black workers cocaine to increase their productivity; small farmers might provide it instead of food and warehouse owners along the lazy big southern state rivers as a substitute for bad wages. The *British Medical Journal* reported that 'some planters kept the drug in stock among the plantation supplies and issued regular rations of cocaine just as they used to issue rations of whisky'.

In the cities in the north, to which many blacks were beginning to migrate in the usually vain hope that they might find better conditions, cocaine was frequently cheaper than alcohol (50 cents in 1900 might buy a whole week's supply). By this year, cocaine could be bought over the counter in drug stores without any form of prescription all across America. It was just as easily bought and sold in the street. Worse, from the point of view of the authorities, cocaine use had slipped downwards into the underworld, light years away from the middle-class salons where it had been so assiduously peddled by respectable medical men, who were quite possibly indulging a little themselves.

Alcoholic drinks, tobacco and opium smoking, all perceived by polite society in both guises, heaven and hell, were as inevitable a part of the underworld which took hold so firmly of nineteenth-century American society as the other great vice, prostitution. Cocaine was merely an addition to the list and was useful on a number of accounts. But slowly, reports began to emerge of both white and black prostitutes 'stupified' by cocaine. There were also reports of 'fiends' who progressed from smoking opium to injecting morphine and thence on to what, in the 1950s, would be known as 'speedballs' of injectable morphine and cocaine. In 1900 more than half the prostitutes in the Fort Worth, Texas, gaol were said to be heavy cocaine users. Consumption, which had remained fairly steady during the period 1885–93, went up by a staggering 500 per cent by 1900; it remained at these levels until 1910. In 1897 it was priced at $2 an ounce, or eight cents a gramme. Even allowing for the massive inflation of the next hundred years, this made the cocaine of the time very inexpensive. It was also generally much purer, as the scam of cutting it with other substances was something waiting to be discovered by a more cost-conscious, demand-driven modern world.

While cocaine was hovering between its debut as the medical wonder of the age and its new persona as the drug of choice of undesirables, racism was on the up, in both the north and south of the country. It had, of course, never really gone away, but the period around the turn of the century saw a large rise in the number of lynchings in the South. The Ku Klux Klan was finding that its recruiting drives were paying dividends. Of all the unlikely candidates, Coca-Cola – along, it has to be said, with other similar products – was dragged willy-nilly into this rising tide of racism by dint of its contents.

In 1898, a zealous Oregon evangelist specifically attacked the drink by name. (It was, of course, the best known. Fame is a two-edged sword – the other side is infamy.) From a pulpit in a town close to Atlanta, he asserted that it contained fully two-thirds cocaine and that this led inexorably onto addiction, as well it might, had the story been even half true. Unsubstantiated rumours like these, however much denied or clearly ludicrous they were, tended to circulate in a climate where food and drink quality was still not controlled. In conjunction with the local prejudices about blacks, seen on the streets drinking Coca-Cola, the results were all too predictable.

By this time, stories were also circulating about an increasing number of black attacks on white employers and rapes by blacks on white women. All of these crimes were reported to have been fuelled by cocaine. In September 1906, there was a major race riot in Atlanta itself, where Coca-Cola was made. It was caused by newspaper reports of black 'cocaine fiends'; the riot was by whites. All through the first decade of the twentieth century, newspapers ran stories like these. The *New York Tribune*, for example, carried an article in which a Georgian complained that Coca-Cola produced 'similar effects to cocaine, morphine and such like. Men become addicted to it.' The *Atlanta Constitution*, in 1901, said: 'Use of the drug [cocaine] among negroes is growing to an alarming extent . . . it is stated that quite a number of the soft drinks dispensed at soda fountains contain cocaine and that these drinks serve to unconsciously cultivate the habit.'

The Coca-Cola Company had moved to take out the cocaine by 1901, but for more reason than that its presence was a danger to social harmony. Asa Candler, the genius behind the Company's success, was acutely tuned in to the prevailing ethos. He could see that cocaine, far from remaining a universal panacea, was, by the turn of the century, becoming a curse. If not quite the 'third scourge of mankind', it was at least not something to put into a fizzy drink sold on the streets. He and other soft drinks manufacturers were beginning to be targeted by medics, not just over-the-top clerics, who argued that the cola drinks were being 'abused' by children as well as adults.

The racial element was also there and there is no doubt that it played a part in ensuring that cocaine came out of Coca-Cola. This proved harder to do than it might appear at first sight. In 1902, a chemical analysis of a sample of Coca-Cola still found 1/400th of a grain of cocaine per ounce of syrup (about .15mg). This was after the Company had produced a leaflet 'What Is it? Coca-Cola, What It Is', in which it was admitted that there was a small quantity of cocaine in the drink. By 1903 it seems certain that the cocaine had all gone, as far as it is ever possible to fully extract a single substance from a complex plant extract. In the same leaflet ('What Is It?') , the writer praised the coca leaf as it 'makes one active, brilliant, vigorous, and able to accomplish great tasks easily'. The Coca-Cola Company remains the biggest buyer of legitimately harvested coca leaf in the world.

It is a measure of the repositioning that had to take place that the 'cocaine in Coke' story now has mythic qualities. Even in 1903, the Company had to tread a line which moved towards a denial that was not a denial. If they had shouted too loudly that the cocaine was now gone, they would have laid themselves open to accusations that they had previously put a harmful product into the drink. Lawsuits would follow, for the United States had already discovered the delights of civil litigation. Equally, the cocaine content had been a major selling point, much promoted, so it would hardly have helped to say too pointedly that the cocaine was now all gone. Curiously, no one seemed to have considered investigating the coca leaves more thoroughly to find out if other alkaloids were as 'beneficial'. The cocaine came out just in time: in 1902 the Georgia state legislature banned any form of cocaine sale as illegal.

The association of drug-taking with a racial minority which could not handle its effects was not new. As well as race, class has always played a major part in the myths surrounding drugs and their use. Some researchers have long suggested that investigation into drug use and racial minorities is misplaced: the real issue has always been, as it remains, one of poverty or social class. In this regard it is worth noting earlier fears voiced about tea and tobacco, and the indolence or rebellion they were likely to inspire in working-class folk in Britain.

In the United States, the first racial group directly to be associated with a drug was the Chinese; that drug was opium. Supply of opium to China, much of it courtesy of British enthusiasm for the trade between its empire in India and the Far East, far exceeded demand by the mid- to late-nineteenth century. Opium was overwhelmingly used by poor Chinese, whether peasant farmers or wage earners in cities. The middle class were not generally big users, if they used it at all. The first wave of Chinese immigrants to America were the dispossessed sons of middle-class families. They came to make their fortunes in the Californian Gold Rush of the 1850s and brought capital to invest, as well as an enthusiasm for making a fortune. They did not, in general, bring opium.

Over time, it became apparent to everyone on the west coast that fortunes were hard to find. As a result, many of the prospectors went out of business or were forced to work for the reducing number of gold-working companies left in the ring. In the growing recession, the Chinese were prepared to acccept lower wages and worse conditions. The seeds of racial conflict were sown.

Between 1862 and 1863 California's gold production fell by more than half. For the next four years, more Chinese left the USA than arrived. But by 1870, those Chinese arriving were poorer and they were prepared to work under even worse conditions. They were, however, often now employed by Chinese from the first wave of immigrants who had been able to survive the conditions and had turned themselves into merchants and suppliers of labour to white-owned companies. A major source of employment was the railway construction industry. The Chinese were also able to supply other services: sex; gambling, to which the Chinese are culturally attracted; and opium.

As the century wore on the British colonial administration in India, worried that their opium monopoly was being undermined by increasing competition from both Persia (modern Iran) and China, had cranked up production in India. Ironically, as the Chinese left the west coast of America to go home, the empty cargo spaces on ships returning from China to the USA were filled with cases of opium. In effect, the opium had been dumped. There was a large increase in opium smoking among the Chinese in California between 1870 and 1880. Because of the prevailing economic conditions, this coincided with growing racial tension. Soon, the age-old connection would be made between a racial minority, crime and the corruption of the (white) majority population, particularly women and the young, by drug-crazed 'fiends'.

Early attacks on opium were not concerned with its harmful nature. Rather, they concentrated on its association with the Chinese and their alien character which, it was claimed, would always make them outsiders, not properly part of America. Opium use was now beginning to spread outside the Chinese community. So-called 'sporting' types began to experiment with it, usually through *demi-monde* contacts. Thus, in classic contagion theory, does a drug spread beyond its habitués.

The city of San Francisco passed a law banning opium dens and the smoking of opium in 1875. A similar law was passed in Virginia City, Nevada, in 1876. These laws were unprecedented at the time; there was no anti-drug legislation in place in America or elsewhere. Nowhere did these laws mention the harm the drug might do to an individual; what was spelled out was merely the danger of the drug's spread. To put this in context, no law was contemplated for alcohol, although public drunkenness was by far the larger problem in the region. As might have been predicted, the passage of these laws created open hostility to the Chinese through what could legitimately be described as official sanction. Race was the key which opened the lock of this Pandora's box, not the contents of the box: opium.

With Southern blacks the situation was quite different, even if the result was predictably similar. Long oppressed, the condition of black people in the old confederacy had not been improved by the Civil War; in many ways their lot worsened. Slavery might have been abolished, but for most the life they had known went on, exacerbated by white taunts about their new-found liberty.

To these insults a further was added in the 1890s when cocaine was going through the first phase of its legal life and employers began to feed cocaine to black workers. Cocaine's breaking out of the medical ghetto had already been presaged by the drug companies, the patent medicine industry and the popular press. By the mid-1890s, the dangers of overuse and death from injudicious application were becoming more widely known among doctors. But for the population at large, cocaine (and by now it *was* cocaine, at least as much as coca) was still much sought after. Cynical use by white employers was inevitable, given the cultural climate; just as inevitable was cocaine's use by prostitutes and criminals. All were part of a larger society in which the drug was still quite legal, openly touted and part of a wide range of products.

The racial element in the subsequent banning of cocaine in the United States played a leading role. Cocaine clearly gave blacks a confidence they might otherwise have lacked. By the early 1900s, what this meant for the white majority was becoming self-evident to those within that majority. In 1903, a Colonel J.W. Watson of Georgia said that 'many of the horrible crimes committed in the Southern States by the coloured people can be traced directly to the cocaine habit'. In 1909 a municipal court judge in Mississippi said that anyone supplying a 'negro' with cocaine was more dangerous than someone who injected a dog with rabies.

In an article written in 1908, Dr Leonard Corning (the inventor of spinal anaesthesia using cocaine) wrote: 'In its use, too, requiring as it does none of the sometimes elaborate paraphernalia associated with the abuse of opium and morphine, it appeals to the most wretched classes of drug victims in the cities, to the negro field hands of the South, as well as to the tramp in his "jungle".' He went on: 'The use of "coke" is probably much more widely spread among negroes than among whites. "Heaven dust" they call it. There is little doubt that every Jew peddler in the South carries the stuff, although many States have lately made its sale a felony.'

By 1910 Dr Hamilton Wright, who figured prominently in the fight to make opium and cocaine illegal, was able confidently to announce: 'Cocaine is often the direct incentive to the crime of rape by the negroes of the South and other sections of the country.' More was to come. Dr Edward Huntington Williams, writing in the *New York Times* in 1914, asserted that 'sexual desires are increased and perverted . . . peaceful negroes become quarrelsome, and timid negroes develop a degree of "Dutch courage" that is sometimes almost incredible'.

By 1914 the arguments had more or less all been won. Cocaine (and opium) were well on their way to being banned by federal law; many states had some time earlier passed laws banning these drugs. But the motives of many were mixed. Dr Williams, for example, was actually an anti-prohibitionist at a time when prohibition was gaining ground. His exaggerated views on cocaine and the 'negro problem' were fuelled by a greater fear that alcohol would be banned; cocaine was talked up by him as the greater of two evils. Dr Williams's article in the *New York Times* was headlined: 'Murder and Insanity Increasing Among Lower Class Because They Have Taken to "Sniffing" Since Being Deprived of Whisky By Prohibition'. It began:

> For some years there have been rumours about the increase in drug taking in the South – vague, but always insistent rumours that the addiction to such drugs as morphine and cocaine was becoming a veritable curse to the coloured race in certain regions. Some of these reports read like the wildest flights of a sensational fiction writer. Stories of cocaine orgies and 'sniffing parties' followed by wholesale murders seem like lurid journalism of the yellowist variety.
>
> In point of fact there was nothing 'yellow' about many of these

> reports. Nine men killed in Mississippi on one occasion by crazed cocaine takers, five in North Carolina, three in Tennessee – these are the facts that need no imaginative colouring. And since this gruesome evidence is supported by the printed records of the insane hospitals, courts, jails and penitentiaries, there is no escaping the conviction that drug taking has become a race menace in certain regions south of the line [the Mason-Dixon line, which separated the states of the North from those of the South].

However, a contemporary study of admissions to the Georgia State Sanitarium from 1909 to 1914, where 2,119 blacks had been admitted, showed that only three had been there for narcotic addiction, and that cocaine was only indicated once. A second patient was admitted for using cocaine, morphine and alcohol to excess. At the same time there were 142 'drug psychoses' among those white patients admitted.

Perhaps the most startling example of racial motivation in the impetus to ban cocaine is demonstrated by the various Southern police forces who demanded larger calibre handguns on the grounds that their ordinary weapons could not stop cocaine-crazed blacks. This belief was also mentioned by Dr Williams. 'The drug produces several other conditions which make the "fiend" a peculiarly dangerous criminal. One of these conditions is a temporary immunity to shock – a resistance to the knockdown effects of fatal wounds.' He insisted: 'Bullets fired into vital parts, that would drop a sane man in his tracks, fail to check the "fiend" – fail to stop his rush or weaken his attack.'

He related the story of the Chief of Police of Asheville, North Carolina, who had been called to a store where a hitherto 'inoffensive negro', whom he knew, was running amok in a 'cocaine frenzy'. When he got there this 'inoffensive negro' stabbed the officer who then shot him in the heart 'but the shot did not even stagger the man'. He saved his ammunition, fearful of other blacks rushing towards him, and finished the job by clubbing the man to death. The next day, reports Dr Williams, 'the Chief exchanged his revolver for one of heavier calibre. And many other officers in the South; who appreciate the increased vitality of the cocaine-crazed negroes, have made similar exchange for guns of greater shocking power for the express purpose of combating the "fiend" when he runs amok.' Thus were .32 police sidearms across the Southern states eventually swapped for the much heavier .38 hand guns still in use today. It seems gratuitous to report that, adding insult to injury, there were many reports that blacks on cocaine were ace pistol shots. This reinforced an informal rule that when confronted by a black the police would shoot first, on the double grounds that he was probably a 'fiend' and as such armed, and liable to be a crack shot.

Cocaine was repeatedly reported to be the drug of choice among blacks, but the linking of this drug with 'abnormal' crimes, in particular rape, is very slender. This did not stop sections of the American press, led on by eminent 'authorities' like Hamilton Wright (who had his own agenda, as we shall shortly see), perpetrating the myth. They simply could not let the story go. Rape, crime and drug addiction, allied to poor blacks, was a potent and explosive mix.

By 1919, though, when 78 blacks were lynched in the South, the menace of the white powder had been overtaken by a bigger red menace – communism. Although many of the lynch mobs who murdered blacks went on the rampage because they believed blacks had raped white women, the enemy was now perceived to be an alien creed. Cocaine, in the troubled history of race relations in America, had played its part. Not until the 1980s would race and drugs re-emerge as an integral package in quite the same way. When it did, it would be in uncannily similar circumstances.

The alien invasion threat to the American way of life was a well-entrenched view by the end of the First World War; isolationism would shortly follow as a foreign policy. There was some rhyme to this, if not a lot of reason. The end of the nineteenth century and the beginning of the twentieth saw the biggest influx of people ever in the United States, largely into the eastern seaboard, and most of all Ellis Island and the port of New York. The Statue of Liberty and all it purportedly stood for notwithstanding, citizens of the United States had some grounds for feeling overwhelmed. The rise of the drugs laws can in part be ascribed to this sense of invasion and a desire to keep what they considered the dark forces of the unknown at bay. It has to be said that the citizens of America were asked to embrace an extraordinary number of people and that they did so for the most part without complaint. Yet the strains that such an influx created were apparent. The underlying motif from this time on was that America was under siege. The isolationalists believed this fervently: if only the United States kept out of world affairs, she could build a fortress within which all the best values known to humankind could be nurtured.

Many of America's citizens carried another torch, a moral certainty born on the back of old-time religion. The moves to ban alcohol were part of a growing wider belief that the American way of life was the only one and that the nation had a moral duty to help the rest of a benighted world re-create these values. It was this view that wove the backcloth of the movement for the banning of opium. And if there were, as ever, more venal economic desires, the moral certainties of this newly born America would ensure they were buried.

The American embrace of cocaine in the 1880s was a symptom of a society in a hurry, ever on the lookout for some means by which the goals of a seemingly ever-expanding economy and even geography, could be fulfilled more quickly. But in the rest of the industrialised world – overwhelmingly European – cocaine never had anything like the same impact, nor were there moves to market its apparent delights. Cultural certainty, too, meant that Europeans still largely looked upon the Americans as brash and largely uncultured, not people whom one would wish to emulate. The faddishness of American pursuits had to be set against the certainties of European attitudes: at this time the European empires of Britain, France, Holland, Austro-Hungary, Belgium, Germany and others were reaching their apogee. *Fin-de-siècle* decadence might allow artists and dilettantes to embrace the odd creed, which might well be attached to certain kinds of drug-taking or other Bohemian behaviour, but there was never going to be an import of an American cultural phenomemon. It would take the horrors of the First World War to change all that when what was left of Europe's belief in itself was mostly shattered. People began to turn to a younger, more vibrant and 'other' set of values to try to make, not sense, but at least an escape.

In Britain there was certainly a market for cocaine, but it never amounted to anything much. At least until 1914, it seems to have been confined to middle-class 'dabbling'. There were tragedies: in 1901 two sisters, Ida and Edith Yeoland, committed suicide by swallowing cocaine. They had been struggling actresses. Cocaine was easy to come by in circumstances such as these, but what evidence exists suggests that its use outside conventional medicine was not concentrated on any sub-group (like actors or actresses, or musicians, let alone criminals). Rather, it seems to have been a problem only where a first medicinal use shaded imperceptibly into dependence. As with the United States, doctors were most exposed to the dangers of overuse.

In Europe cocaine also had a low profile; it was in fairly frequent use in pre-war Vienna, but with that city's reputation for being the most decadent capital in Europe, that should not surprise. Overall, it was the American experience with cocaine that took the centre stage.

6

PANIC ON THE STREETS: THE RISE AND RISE OF THE DRUGS LAWS

BEFORE 1907 DRUGS LIKE COCAINE, opium or morphine could be bought over the counter in pharmacies in the United States, just like other goods; a similar situation applied in Europe. Much of the cocaine consumed by Americans, as we have seen, was as an ingredient contained within a patent medicine. Manufacturers did not have to disclose the contents of these preparations – the term *patent* medicine is derived from this; that is, a concoction protected by patent law. With the power of the patent medicine industry allied to that of the pharmaceutical companies, it was always going to be hard to find the right kind of law to protect the consumer. By 1900 there were any number of local and state laws aimed at curbing the worst practices, but they were often ineffective and rarely applied. At the same time it was believed that any attempt to pass a federal law, which might have curbed the worst excesses of manufacturers and retailers, and would have certainly created a uniform set of rules, would be unconstitutional.

It took the efforts of a number of individuals to change all this. The result was eventually the passage of what has become the 'root' law on drugs in the United States. This represented the beginning of America's lead – which still applies – in the global fight to prevent drugs from becoming widely available and widely used. Nearly nine decades have passed since that first federal law, and it is clear that the approach contained within it has led to a comprehensive failure of drugs control. From a situation in which drug use and abuse was relatively insignificant – even when cocaine was legally available in many forms only a very small percentage of Americans ever took it – we have reached a point where many more drugs are much more widely available and used by ever-increasing numbers of people.

Since 1900 the biggest change has been a shift in the supply side, from legitimate sources to criminal ones. It is arguable that this shift was created by the same law designed to prevent drug use and abuse. It is clear that the law represented a shift away from a medical model, in which abuse was perceived a treatable condition, towards a prohibitive model in which abuse was seen to be a social problem and therefore potentially punishable. The impact of this shift cannot be over-emphasised, as it has affected so much of what has happened since in both national and international policy, and law on drug use.

The man who began the process which would lead to a federal drugs law was Dr Harvey Washington Wiley, the first head of the US Bureau of Chemistry. Ever since he arrived in Washington DC in 1883, Wiley had campaigned against food (and other edible product) adulteration. By 1902 he had brought together a group of young scientists as his so-called 'poison' squad; in effect they acted as human guinea pigs in tests for food additives. The various experiments they took part in were highly publicised but largely devoid of any method. Coca-Cola became one of their later targets when Wiley convinced himself that the caffeine contained within it was dangerous. He believed it to be a major contribution to Cola-Cola's 'malign influence' on American youth as well as its black population.

Before this crusade, Wiley had had his first great triumph in the passage, in 1906, of the federal Food and Drugs Act. There had been over 200 prior attempts to get an act of this kind on the statute books. All had been killed off by a combination of the food, drinks and proprietary medicines industries, but by the early 1900s public opinion was beginning to swing in favour of an enforceable legal requirement to label food and drink. A large measure of this change came about because of the pioneering efforts of journalists like Samuel Hopkins Adams and writers like Upton Sinclair. It had been, it will be recalled, the patent medicine manufacturers who had helped pay in large measure for the expansion of the newspapers and magazines (through myriad advertisements) which now turned against them. In a series of articles in *Collier's* magazine, in the autumn of 1905, Adams launched a series of devastating attacks against the patent medicine industry and its claims. Upton Sinclair, meanwhile, published his novel *The Jungle*, which detailed the gory, not to say gothic, horrors of the meat-processing business.

Adams's first article dealt with the so-called 'red clause' by which an advertising contract for patent medicines was voided if hostile laws were passed. Until that time, this ensured that the press always came out against controls. At the time Adams was writing, newspapers and magazines had an expanding revenue base; further across the country an increasingly sophisticated and aware public was demanding some form of action. In all this, Dr Wiley was a tireless campaigner, criss-crossing the country to lobby, brief and cajole. When the Pure Food and Drugs Act was passed in June 1906, it was immediately given the soubriquet 'Dr Wiley's Law'.

The new law was a curious animal. It insisted on the labelling of foodstuffs and drinks, but made no distinction as to their safety or not. And Wiley had some highly idiosyncratic ideas as to what might or might not be 'safe', even if this concept was not covered by the Act. There is plenty of evidence to suggest he was specifically after the Coca-Cola Company, who added saccharin – another one of Wiley's targets – to their products before 1906. After this time, ever mindful of their image, they removed it. But by then Wiley had switched his attack onto the drink's caffeine content as another dangerous substance. Wiley's philosophy was one which had at its heart a moral purpose. The consumer had to be told the truth: lying was the ultimate sin. His attack on Coca-Cola, he said, was due to the fact that people did not necessarily know that it contained caffeine (unlike tea or coffee, of which this was publicly known). He said: 'The injury to public health is the least important question and should be considered last of all. The real evil of food adulteration is deception of the consumer.'

In the most bizarre twist of all, a case was finally mounted against Coca-Cola for *failing* to contain cocaine, despite the implication in the name that it had to be an integral part of the formula. Wiley naturally believed he had found the Achilles heel in this prosecution. He believed that Coca-Cola would be found guilty as a matter of fact in the courts and punished by their public, who would realise their fast-becoming favourite soft drink was a fraud. Wiley's attacks on the Coca-Cola Company have all the hallmarks of a vendetta, but he may simply have kept after them because they were so prominent. In effectively bringing them to book, Wiley would be making an unanswerable case in favour of his law.

The Coca-Cola Company eventually won their case after a long and arduous fight through the courts. With one thing and another, it is possible to understand the current sensitivity the Company maintains with regard to its history, its formulae and how it is marketed. For example, after the debacle over caffeine and its possible harmful effect on children, no child under the age of 12 appeared in a Coca-Cola advertisement until the late 1980s.

The crusade against adulterated food and drink was the beginning of a much larger series of campaigns. One of these campaigns would lead eventually to alcohol prohibition, aimed at cleaning up the country and its worst habits, both in manufacture and consumption. Drug use, such as the use of cocaine, was now spreading outwards and downwards into a wider range of American society and was increasingly associated with crime. It was the next target.

While cocaine was seen to be a problem, the bigger problem was perceived to be opium, to the extent that for a while America believed itself to have a worse opium problem than China. Among the leading lights who espoused this view was Dr Hamilton Wright.

Wright became the US Opium Commissioner (an early version of the American and British drugs tsars of the 1990s) in 1908. He was not particularly well qualified for this role. Nor was one of the other leading campaigners for international controls on drugs at that time, Bishop Brent, based in Manila, the capital of the Philippines. Apart from any domestic problems with drugs, the United States had inherited a foreign one, particularly in the Philippines, taken from Spain after the end of the short-lived Spanish–American War. This annexation resulted in the USA becoming a colonial power.

Under the robust leadership of Theodore Roosevelt, America was going through a series of profound changes. Among them was the huge level of immigration and the annexation of a number of territories like Cuba, as well as the Philippines which had what was believed to be a serious opium smoking problem. Apart from this, there was a growing realisation that the British and their empire might shortly become the biggest obstacle to the American economy reaching its full potential. The biggest untapped market for the United States at that time was China. The moral issues posed by the opium smokers of the Philippines would be combined with this desire to break into the Chinese market, creating a climate whereby Christian duty could happily sit with economic necessity.

China also had a 'moral' problem, opium smoking, one which the USA now came to understand much better through what had been uncovered in the Philippines. Apart from their direct knowledge there, the extent of the Chinese problem was relayed back home through the many thousands of American missionaries in China. All identified the villain of the piece as Britain with its huge opium-growing industry, largely to be found in India.

The United States began to press for an international conference on opium and opium traffic. It was aided by the Brussels Convention of 1890, which had dealt with slave and drink traffic in Africa. The USA was also encouraged in the view that if the opium trade could be curbed, its own problems with this particular drug at home might be alleviated. It had made direct representations to the Empress of China, who was vehemently against opium use, in the expectation that if all went well the USA would be well placed to lever its way into the Chinese economy.

The British, with their Indian economy heavily implicated in the opium business, had not gone out of their way to cooperate before the 1900s. In 1905, however, a Liberal government was elected and in 1906 the House of Commons unanimously adopted a resolution 'that this House reaffirms its conviction that the Indo-Chinese opium traffic is morally indefensible, and requests His Majesty's government to take such steps as may be necessary for bringing it to a speedy close'. As a result of this pious intent negotiations between the British and Chinese began; the British finally agreed to reduce, then halt, all opium imports into China within ten years.

Encouraged by the turn of events the United States finally convened the first international conference on opium, appropriately enough in Shanghai, in 1909; thirteen countries attended. The missing producer country was Turkey, which, although being an important source of opium, was going through a period of intense internal unrest. The agreement that the attending nations hammered out of the Shanghai Conference was for much greater cooperation and control of opium, morphine and heroin (which hardly figured yet as a serious problem). Further, it was agreed to reconvene the conference with plenipotentiary powers at the Hague in 1911, with a view to control even more strictly the production, distribution and sale specifically of opium.

The two years between these conferences saw frantic efforts by Hamilton Wright and others in the United States to get domestic legislation passed, both to back up the international agreements in the pipeline and to demonstrate the seriousness with which the United States took the issue of drugs control. By late 1909 Wright had a plan drawn up which would control drugs through the tax system: if passed, his proposed Act would require every drug dealer to register, pay a small tax and record all transactions. Wright believed that the best way for this system to work would be through the individual states, not the federal government.

His Bill was eventually introduced to Congress by David Foster, the representative from Vermont. The Foster Bill was framed to ensure disclosure of all traffic in opiates, cocaine, chloral hydrate and cannabis, no matter how small the quantities. The Bill was eventually defeated through a mixture of the same forces which had opposed legislation on the labelling of food and drink. Wright had argued very strongly that, for instance, imports of crude opium into the USA had risen far more rapidly than the population. He suggested, too, that the pharmaceutical and medical professions were untrustworthy and that chemists were indiscriminately selling addictive drugs, along with many doctors who were happy to prescribe them. Those same druggists, through the National Wholesale Druggists' Association, told the congressional hearing on the Bill that although they could see the point of including opium, morphine and cocaine, cannabis ought to be left out. More importantly, they argued that all *patent* medicines should be left out. They also added that the Bill, if passed, would lead to a huge bureaucratic shambles which would place intolerable financial strains on all of their businesses.

Hamilton Wright, in his evidence, chose to attack cola soda pops: 'What about this material they call Coca-Cola?' he asked. He demanded that coca leaves be included under the Bill, since the colas were made from them: 'Coca-cola . . . and all those things that are sold to Negroes all over the south.' He also declared himself embarrassed at the amount of opium the United States appeared to be consuming, a point he made a little later in an article in the *New York Times* of 12 March 1911, headlined 'Uncle Sam is the worst drug fiend in the world'. He was bylined as the 'US Opium Commissioner, 44 years old, and preparing for the Hague Conference'. He wrote:

> Of all the nations of the world, the United States consumes most habit-forming drugs per capita. Opium, the most pernicious drug known to humanity, is surrounded, in this country, with far fewer safeguards than any other nation in Europe fences it with . . . few people realise how serious the opium habit has become in the United States . . . our prisons and our hospitals are full of victims of it, it has robbed ten thousand businessmen of moral sense and made them beasts who prey upon their fellows.

He suggested that opium consumption in the United States at that time was more than the combined total for Russia, Austria-Hungary, Germany,

Holland and Italy (combined population, 155 million, as against the US population of 90 million). He claimed the United States was using half a million pounds weight of opium against their combined total of just 40,000 pounds.

> And opium is not the only habit-forming drug we are called upon to fight. I am not far wrong in stating that we have the largest per capita consumption of narcotics and anodynes of any people in the world. Take the question of cocaine, for instance. It is a generally known fact that during the past twenty years cocaine has been diverted from its original use by the surgeon as a local anaesthetic to pander to the supposed needs of large numbers of our population. It is estimated, after a wide consultation, that 15,000 [425 kilogrammes] or 20,000 ounces [570 kilogrammes] of this drug are sufficient to satisfy the demands of surgery in the United States. Today there are manufactured in the States at least 150,000 ounces [4,250 kilogrammes] of the drug, the larger part of which is put to improper uses.
>
> It is the unanimous opinion of every State and municipal organisation . . . that the misuse of cocaine is direct incentive to crime; that it is perhaps of all factors a singular one in augmenting the criminals' ranks. The illicit use of the drug is most difficult to cope with, and the habitual use of it temporarily raises the power of a criminal to a point where in resisting arrest there is no hesitation to murder.

And, taking up the theme we have already examined, he continued:

> It is really more appalling in its effect than any other habit-forming drug in use in the United States. In the South the use of cocaine among the lower order of working negroes is quite common. It is current knowledge throughout the South that on many public works, levee and railroad construction, and in other working camps where large numbers of negroes congregate, cocaine is peddled pretty openly. In all our large cities the drug is compounded with low grades of spirit, which make a maddening compound. Inquiries have shown that contractors of labour in the South under the impression that cocaine

WHITE MISCHIEF

stimulates the negro labourers to a greater output of work, wink at the distribution of the drug to them. There is no doubt that this drug, perhaps more than any other, is used by those concerned in the white slave traffic to corrupt young girls, and that when the habit of using the drug has been established, it is but a short time before such girls fall to the ranks of prostitution.

To illustrate the insidious spread of the cocaine habit, you should know that an ever-increasing number of our sailors and soldiers are falling into the use of it. It was found recently that some of the Legation guards at Peking were cocaine fiends, and the Chinese government found it necessary to ask the treaty powers to permit her to prohibit the importation of cocaine except for medicinal purposes. India is also threatened with the vice. *But the United States is pre-eminently the country in which there is an abuse of cocaine* [my emphasis].

This gives a flavour of Hamilton Wright's crusade; his triumph was to be in the passage of the Harrison Act a few years after this article appeared. The Foster Bill was finally thrown out in 1911, despite the best efforts of Wright and Dr Wiley. Wiley had wanted a much more draconian act, one which would have banned caffeine, his old target. In effect, the Bill was killed by the legal drugs and pharmacists' trade. They had a point: had this Bill been passed the life of the average pharmacist would have been made impossible.

Thwarted by Congress, Hamilton Wright turned to the Hague Conference only to find that there, too, others were intent on spoiling his plans. Britain, Germany, and Holland were all trying to stall on reconvening. Wright was so enraged by this that when the Dutch ambassador was on holiday in Maine he went to see him, threatening that if something were not done the United States would do its utmost to get the conference moved to Washington. He further sought out the British ambassador in Washington to give him a similar earbashing.

The International Conference on Opium opened at the Hague on 1 December 1911. Both Bishop Brent and Hamilton Wright attended; Brent had had to work hard to smooth the choppy waters Wright had stirred. His attitude, that all the other countries were out to sabotage the morally correct and therefore unassailable American position, had so antagonised the other members that Bishop Brent had at one point asked him to give up his anti-drugs campaigning for the sake of the same. Wright had refused point blank.

The conference, attended this time by only twelve nations, spent a long time wrangling over a number of issues which individual countries had hoped would not be raised. The British chose to demand action over cocaine and morphine, no doubt angered by the American attacks on the India-China opium trade which they now claimed was under control and rapidly in decline. The Germans were extremely anxious to protect their by now powerful chemical and pharmaceutical industry (which, among a dizzy array of new drugs, had given the world diacetyl morphine, or heroin, a mere fifteen years earlier). The Portuguese, Dutch and French were each, for their own reasons, protective of their share of the opium trade. The Japanese, playing a card they would use time and again between the wars, professed ignorance of their assistance in the import of both morphine and the syringes for its delivery into China.

For the crusading Americans, the worst aspect of the conference was its refusal to endorse their position. The baseline for the other 11 nations was that 12 countries could hardly make law for the estimated 46 who should have been there if all countries with an interest in the drugs trade had turned up. The United States delegation was considerably weakened in its stance by not having any legislation in place at home. But they could take some comfort in the final conference document, which called in Chapter Three for control of all phases of the preparation and distribution of cocaine, medicinal opium, morphine, heroin and any new derivative that could scientifically be shown to offer similar dangers.

Another conference was set for 1913, to report on progress; yet another for 1914, but the latter was swept away by the larger events of that summer. International concern over drugs control would wait many years and be rekindled in very different circumstances. Meanwhile, in the United States, Hamilton Wright pressed on with his campaign. He was determined that the USA would not return to the international stage (in 1913) without its own legislation on narcotics.

Hamilton Wright's efforts were still backed by Dr Wiley and many others. But he was opposed by a formidable array of interested parties: pharmaceutical companies, like Parke-Davis; the huge array of patent and other proprietary medicine makers and retailers; and by most doctors, who foresaw a time when their prescribing powers would be heavily circumscribed and, worse, their clinical judgement constantly questioned.

The imminent legislation, now under the wing of the Democrat Francis

Harrison, was in most respects the same Bill that had failed in 1911. It forced the various opposed interest groups into action. In October 1912, the American Pharmaceutical Association (APA) met in Denver to call for a forum of all the parties who would be affected. In January 1913 the National Drug Trade Conference (NDTC) was set up; all those who joined were opposed to the Bill. It included the APA, of course, along with the National Association of Medicinal Products, the National Association of Retail Druggists and the National Wholesale Druggists' Association. The American Medical Association (AMA) was also represented.

At the first meeting with Hamilton Wright and Francis Harrison things went badly. Wright became so annoyed that he walked out, while Harrison committed the gaffe of saying he had to leave early to go to the theatre with his wife, adding injudiciously that were he to be late, 'She would fear I had taken an overdose of narcotics.' This confrontational meeting did result in a resolution of a kind. Harrison was to insist that Wright redrafted parts of the Bill to placate the NDTC; as a result, opposition to the Bill was gradually, if painfully, reduced.

The American Medical Association had also to be squared, for different reasons. First formed in 1847, it had long been a small organisation with its members largely drawn from the east coast. But membership of the AMA had increased from 8,500 in 1900 to over 36,000 in 1913 and it was fast becoming a powerful force both for the improved education of doctors and for their status. Part of the changes being wrought meant that the AMA had got far more closely involved in politics, and with the lobbying of Congress. At the same time, it was anxious that the profession maintained a correct distance from government both at federal and state levels.

The American situation with regard to the onset of drugs legislation was being mirrored elsewhere, but for all the reasons outlined here the Harrison Act has come to symbolise the shift in drugs policies worldwide. Its importance can hardly be overstated. Although there was a drug addiction problem in both Europe and the United States during the nineteenth century, it was the cocaine craze and not the penchant for opium or morphine which first set the reformers ablaze. Ostensibly it was Bishop Brent's report on the opium problem America inherited from Spain in the Philippines which gave people like Hamilton Wright, an amateur meddler if ever there was one, his *cause célèbre*. But behind both stood the physically massive presence of Dr Wiley with his eccentric views on scientific research and his obsessions with saccharine and caffeine, among other additives. Behind these men were many upright American citizens anxious to ban the demon of all demons, alcohol, which they saw as the real target. It is a particular irony that Hamilton Wright, who had angered many of those who came across him by his manner, would get his come-uppance for his own drink problem. It eventually cost him his job.

The Harrison Act marks a change in attitude towards all drugs: it provided the anti-alcohol brigade with a handle on which to lean for prohibition, which they would get a few years later. It also meant that, for the first time, the illegal manufacture and distribution of drugs would, in a curious sense, be legitimised. We live with the consequences of that to this day.

In 1913, during the debates about the proposed Act, there were other conflicts. Many were only just beneath the surface but constantly threatening to burst forth: for instance, the conflict between the drugs manufacturers and retailers on the one hand and the doctors on the other. The doctors had long fought a battle to stop what they considered to be their absolute prerogative: the issue of prescription drugs, a category in which they wished to include more or less everything that could be called medicine. For their part the druggists believed, with some justification, that the doctors wanted an absolute monopoly, in which druggists merely did their masters' bidding. The consumer figured not at all in this debate, wishing only for cures at a time when few were available with any certainty. Drug users, as ever, sought the cheapest supply for their habit, be it chronic or acute.

The main batttleground over which the Harrison Bill came to be fought was the degree to which the federal government could insist on the detail of the records which were being proposed. The Bill's thrust was not to ban drugs like cocaine or morphine, but to tax them. This was the background to what would become the Harrison Narcotic Act. Among the chief proponents of the Bill in government was the US Secretary of State, William Jennings Bryan, a man of deep prohibitionist convictions. He urged that the Bill be passed to fulfil the American obligations under the 1912 Hague Convention. Senator Mann (of Mann Act fame: one of the key federal laws which paved the way for federal law in general) also suggested that international law demanded the Bill be passed.

When it was finally passed in December 1914, in a few minutes, it could reasonably be argued that the eyes of Congress were elsewhere. They were, as ever, looking at alcohol prohibition.

The anti-drugs law was seen more as a tidying of the legal position than as part of a great moral international crusade, as Wright and Wiley had argued. A week after the Bill was passed, a huge demonstration took place in Washington in support of the real goal of many Americans: the ban on alcohol. If drug use had been seen as part of an attack on the (white) American way of life, which the Chinese were corrupting with opium, the black attacking under the influence of cocaine and the Hispanic undermining with marijuana, alcohol cut through all racial barriers and undermined everyone and everything. The image of the saloon bar was a powerful one. It was easy enough to witness the reality in every city, town and settlement: it attracted white, black, yellow and every other colour and race. The immigrants, still pouring into the country, were singled out as the most vulnerable to temptation. But concern for their welfare was less prominent than the idea that drink led them to commit more of the crimes for which they were already in general blamed.

The size of the anti-alcohol lobby may be judged from the fact that a petition of six million signatures accompanied the demonstration – the largest ever. The vote was lost. Three years later, when the USA was a participant in the First World War and thoughts about the dangers of drink undermining morale were prominent, Congress passed the Eighteenth Amendment, outlawing the manufacture, sale and transportation of alcohol into or out of the United States. Prohibition, which falls outside the remit of this book, led to a huge increase in criminality, murder and mayhem. Its eventual demise might, however, be noted. Alcohol was as ubiquitous a drug in America as it was elsewhere in the world. If anything, the attempt to ban it is suggestive of that same 'America as a fortress' attitude which, from time to time, overrides a more balanced and realistic approach.

On the face of it the Harrison Bill did not appear to be a prohibition law at all. Its title said: 'An Act to provide for the registration of, with collectors of internal revenue, and to impose a special tax upon all persons who produce, import, manufacture, compound, deal in, dispense, sell, distribute, or give away opium or coca leaves, their salts, derivatives, or preparations, and for other purposes.' The Act set up a licensing system. The patent medicine manufacturers were exempt if they produced goods with no more than two grains (125mg) of opium, or more than a quarter grain of morphine, an eighth grain of heroin, in each ounce (28 grammes) of the preparation. In theory the Act merely regulated a hitherto unregulated trade and, indeed, it specifically said that doctors had the right to prescribe what they saw fit to patients.

Unfortunately, or perhaps not, there was no recognition in the Act that addiction of any form, physical or psychological, was a treatable condition. Doctors who subsequently treated addicts with preparations of cocaine, heroin or morphine were acting outside the law. At a stroke the Act created a whole new class of criminal, drove the supply (and later the manufacture) of these drugs underground and paved the way for the international crisis in drugs and drugs trafficking we have today.

The actual effects of the Harrison Act, which came into force in April 1915, were noted by the *New York Medical Journal* in May 1915:

> As was expected . . . the immediate effects of the Harrison antinarcotic law were seen in the flocking of habitués to hospitals and sanitoriums. Sporadic crimes of violence were reported too, due to the usually desperate efforts by addicts to obtain drugs, but occasionally to a delirious state induced by sudden withdrawal.

Six months later, in the journal *American Medicine*, an editorial suggested:

> Narcotic drug addiction is one of the gravest and most important questions confronting the medical profession today. Instead of improving conditions, the laws recently passed have made the problem more complex. Honest medical men have found such handicaps and dangers to themselves and their reputations in these laws . . . that they have decided to have as little to do as possible with drug addicts or their needs . . . The druggists are in the same position and for similar reasons many of them have discontinued entirely the sale of narcotic drugs. [The addict] is denied the medical care he urgently needs, open, above-board sources from which he formerly obtained his drug supply are closed to him, and he is driven to the underworld where he can get his drug, but of course, surreptitiously and in violation of the law.

In 1926 the *Illinois Medical Journal* concluded:

> The Harrison Narcotic law should never have been placed upon the Statute books of the the United States. It is to be granted that the well-meaning blunderers who put it there had in mind only the idea of making it impossible for addicts to secure their supply of 'dope' and to

prevent unprincipled people from making fortunes, and fattening upon the infirmities of their fellow men.

As is the case with most prohibitive laws, however, this one fell far short of the mark. So far, in fact, that instead of stopping the traffic, those who deal in dope now make double their money from the poor unfortunates upon whom they prey.

By 1936 a former chief of police in Berkeley, California, August Vollmer, was writing:

> Stringent laws, spectacular police drives, vigorous prosecutions and imprisonment of addicts and peddlers have proved not only useless and enormously expensive as a means of correcting this evil, but they are also unjustifiably and unbelievably cruel in their application to the unfortunate drug victims. Repression has driven this vice underground and produced the narcotics smugglers and supply agents, who have grown wealthy out of this evil practice and who, by devious methods, have stimulated traffic in drugs. Finally, and not the least of the evils associated with repression, the helpless addict has been forced to resort to crime in order to get money for the drug which is absolutely indispensable for his comfortable existence.
>
> Drug addiction, like prostitution and like liquor, is not a police problem; it never has been and never can be solved by policemen. It is first and last a medical problem, and if there is a solution it will be discovered not by policemen, but by scientifically and competently trained medical experts whose sole objective will be the reduction and possible eradication of this devastating appetite.

By this time the road on which the rest of the world, not just the USA, was destined to follow to its bitter end was well established. The end of the First World War had seen the setting up – very much at the insistence of the USA – of the League of Nations, a body which the United States then refused to join. As part of its early remit, the League took over the Hague Convention on narcotics. At the first meeting an advisory committee on opium and other drugs, including cocaine, had been set up. It had two jobs: to collect and analyse information on drug traffic; and to try to get agreement from all the member states to adhere to the rules agreed by the Convention. The problem, which we will explore in more detail in the next chapter, was that the conflicting interests of the contracting countries and of the manufacturers of drugs within those countries would blow any chance of a coherent policy out of the water. Of all the countries most implicated in the cocaine, opium and heroin trades, Japan stands out and deserves a detailed if uncomfortable examination. The British, who had finally, in the First World War, to make cocaine and opium illegal as drugs (and not just frame the law by suggesting they were poisons), were as ambiguous as ever over their part in the opium trade. The trade still had a huge impact on the Indian economy (that is, it still provided significant revenue to the government there). Germany, although the loser in the recent war, was as anxious as ever to protect its highly successful chemical industry. The Dutch had an interest in both opium and coca production in Java and the Swiss were happy to accommodate those who wished to use its secretive banking system to launder legally made drugs, which were to disappear into the system.

We have now come to the watershed in the more general history of drugs and drug-taking. The period between the first Hague Convention, the American Harrison Act, the tidying up of the law in wartime Britain and the onset of the League and the post-Second World War world saw a transition between a system of drug production which was largely regulated by legally based companies and the governments under whose jurisdiction they fell, and the rise of entirely illegal operations. These were always present, just like the practice of creaming off coca leaves or opium from legal shipments. But what began to happen from the 1920s was a new industry. It might be seen to have started with prohibition in the United States. It was certainly helped in Asia by the entirely cynical trade carried on under the counter by the Japanese, with almost absolute collusion from their government.

More than anything, and something which is often forgotten, the illegal drugs business depends on consumers willing to seek out the dealer and to break the law on their own account. The experience of prohibition ought amply to have demonstrated the extent to which law-abiding citizens would be prepared to do so. The key point to be made is that it was legal manufacturers of drugs like cocaine who acted as the first dealers. They, along with doctors and pharmacists, created a demand which, in the case of cocaine, was entirely absent before the drug was isolated from the leaf (coca leaves might well be in use in all kinds of products across the world today had cocaine not been discovered).

The business of supply of both coca leaf and cocaine had become a well-established one by the time the Harrison Act was passed, and other laws on drugs use across the world followed. Both growers of the leaf and manufacturers of cocaine were reluctant to end their trade and for a while the supply of now illegal cocaine could only come from these sources. Apparently flying in the face of any law of consumer demand, as the original supply diminished demand for illicit cocaine did not grow; it died away. The first great cocaine boom had been a small but integral part of the American era of Boosterism, that great expansive period at the end of the nineteenth century. That period could be said to have lasted until the First World War. The inter-war years saw a pattern of bust rather than boom. It would take the great economic boom in America, which has lasted more or less continuously since 1945, for another boom in drugs use to begin. Then, as before, it would coincide with a shift in social perception and attitude.

PART THREE

COCAINE CENTURY

7

MAKING DOLLARS, PASSING THE BUCK

UP UNTIL THE 1880S, the history of coca and cocaine remains fairly easy to follow. By the time cocaine had moved from being a curiosity to a cure-all and thence to near-catastrophic status in the minds of many, the picture becomes far more complicated. As we have seen, it was the American experience with cocaine which alarmed and then stampeded the authorities there into acting to introduce anti-drugs law. Their anxieties swept away the chances of a rational debate. Cocaine was demonised very quickly; excluding its use by the public, medicine had found out to its cost that this was an unpredictable drug whose effects could vary alarmingly between patients. A lethal dose was hard to predict, as indeed was its effectiveness. What might attract a casual user – its capacity for mood shifting – was precisely its danger for a medical establishment seeking consistency.

While these facts were bearing in on users, suppliers were still manufacturing the drug in quantities which well exceeded official demand. Growers, too, in a number of places round the world had been encouraged by the wave of demand from the United States. From the turn of the nineteenth century into the twentieth, in order to unpack the story we have to be prepared to look in many places, over a lengthy period of time. The coca leaf escaped its South American heartland just as cocaine moved more decisively into Europe – and Asia. If cocaine remains a quintessentially American drug, then its story is as much to do with the progression of the United States in the twentieth century.

The period between the explosive discovery of cocaine in the mid-1880s and its effective demise as part of the limited medical arsenal available before antibiotics lasted hardly longer than a generation – around thirty years. By then the Harrison Act was in force, a world war was being fought and doctors had by and large dismissed cocaine's medicinal properties in favour of other, less volatile and much safer drugs. But cocaine had made its mark on a much wider public and demand for it as a recreational drug would continue in fits and starts until it made its second major entrance in the 1970s.

Within the period of cocaine's debut, a whole industrial infrastructure had been set up, allied to a huge increase in the production of the leaf in South America. Governments, in alliance with the responsible authorities in medicine and pharmacy alike, were moving in public towards the ostensible elimination of the 'third scourge'. There would, however, from now on always be an ambiguity between public policy and reality. By the 1980s, a hundred years away from the cocaine mania set off in part by Sigmund Freud, that ambiguity would lead to one senior part of the United States government effectively engaging in drug dealing, whilst other parts of the same government were fighting the illegal drugs trade.

In the ostensibly more innocent era of the early twentieth century ,pharmaceutical companies, often in covert if not overt collusion with their governments, manufactured quantities of cocaine which could only ever have been destined for a clandestine if not yet an illegal market. By the 1930s, when cocaine was on the A list of illegal drugs worldwide, the Japanese government actively engaged in every form of illegal drugs dealing in an attempt to assist the financing of its warlike ambitions. Some might perceive the same intention, if not motive, in the USA's antics during the Iran-Contra affair; plus ça change . . .

As with the British in India and the opium trade, cocaine was a drug which colonial governments like the Dutch in Java or Peru believed could boost entire economies. With Peru, this did become the case: for many years the country was the world's single largest source of coca leaf and cocaine paste. In 1900 Peru was supplying around one million tonnes of coca, mainly to the USA, France and Germany. Five years later it sold up to 10 tonnes of cocaine paste (cocaine sulphate) each year to the same sources.

Three of the major players in this early phase in the northern hemisphere were Angelo Mariani, who was only after the coca leaf; Merck of Germany; and Parke-Davis of the United States. Sigmund Freud's role, already remarked upon, was also important although less as an economic force and more as a promoter of cocaine. Freud promoted cocaine as some form of miracle cure-all; he also, in a curious incident redolent of farce, promoted American cocaine over German. The farcical element derives from Freud's own method of approach to the subject. In *Über Coca*, the first scientific paper he quotes to back up his belief in cocaine is the *Therapeutic Gazette*. This was in fact a promotional organ produced by Parke-Davis, the American manufacturers. It was in this publication that Freud read that coca extract had been used to cure morphine addiction; it is an irony that he interpreted this to mean cocaine. In *Über Coca* Freud specifically mentions the Parke-Davis formula. After Freud's paper had been published, Parke-Davis quoted from it. Needless to say, they did not mention that Freud's original praises had been delivered after he had read their own marketing literature.

The plot thickened further when Freud later took a payment from Parke-Davis for directly endorsing their product as cheaper than that obtainable in Vienna, to the lasting fury of Merck in Germany. Merck acidly pointed out that their cocaine was not, in fact, more expensive. Freud, of course, had used up a month's salary in first obtaining his cocaine from Merck, and clearly it still rankled.

Cocaine was expensive at this time (the late 1880s), but from the moment it seemed as if it were to be accepted as the wonder drug of the age, huge efforts went into increasing the supply of the leaves and ensuring that they travelled rather better. Great efforts were put as well into seeking out new sources of supply and possible other locations where the leaves might be grown.

Merck had begun to produce cocaine shortly after Niemann synthesised it but, as noted, in very small quantities, as demand early on had hardly been brisk. The Merck family had been in the pharmaceutical business for centuries. When the new science of alkaloid chemistry emerged in the early nineteenth century, it was natural that they would be at the forefront of its development. Morphine was Merck's first major product, in their list from the 1830s, as was codeine and quinine. Cocaine production began in 1862, but as demand early on was nearly non-existent they were only making about half a kilo a year, probably in order to retain their position as a comprehensive supplier of alkaloid drugs.

On the other side of the Atlantic, Parke-Davis was founded in Detroit in the year Merck began cocaine production, originally as a pharmacy. Its founder was a Dr Duffield. After an early and not very successful start, it was eventually taken over, by first Parke and then George Davis. Duffield shortly after returned to the practice of medicine. George Davis was not only a rich man; he understood, much like Mariani, the importance of advertising in an increasingly crowded market. He and Parke also understood that what the industry lacked was a reliable range of products. Doctors ordering drugs at this time could never be sure that one batch would not contain a totally different quantity or quality of a drug from the next.

As well as emphasising quality control, Parke-Davis also set out to emulate Merck in their range of alkaloid drugs. They sponsored expeditions to seek out possible new products (like guarana and eucalyptus). In 1875 they introduced an extract made from coca; the year after the Parke-Davis Company began to make a profit. The *Therapeutic Gazette* was part of the marketing strategy; it was a reference to the coca elixir and morphine addiction in it that Freud lighted upon. Eventually Parke-Davis, fired up by their own promotional beliefs and the reinforcement of them from doctors like Freud, brought out a whole range of cocaine-based products, including a kit for injecting cocaine directly. It consisted of 300mg of powdered cocaine divided into five capsules, a solution for dissolving the powder, a camel brush and a syringe, and retailed for about $2. At one point they tried to compete with Coca-Cola by starting a soft drink manufacture; they already produced a coca wine.

All this activity, along with the many European and other smaller American firms trying to get in on the act, created a supply problem. When Parke-Davis realised that cocaine was going to be, for however long, the most sought-after drug, they commissioned one of their own chemists, Henry Rusby, to go to Bolivia to see how the supply of coca might be increased. Rusby's expedition reads like a *Boys' Own* adventure. The ship he sailed on from New York, the SS *Acapulco*, was beset by bad weather. At one point a passenger was washed overboard only to be swept back by a following sea. When he eventually reached Panama, where he disembarked, Rusby set out through the isthmus, along the coast of Colombia, Ecuador and Peru, until he reached La Paz in Bolivia. There, he recruited two Texan outlaws (somewhat sadly, given the overall tenor of his journey, not Butch Cassidy and the Sundance Kid) and an Indian guide to set off down the Amazon.

Rusby did uncover new sources of coca but, far more importantly, he changed the rules of the game entirely by experimenting with a process by which coca leaves could be turned into a semi-refined product. In so doing he nearly blew up the hotel room in which he conducted his experiments, which involved setting up an alcohol still. The process he devised is now generally credited to a Peruvian chemist called Alfredo Bignon. It is still part of the method used in illegal operations today to manufacture crude cocaine. The crude paste, locally called *buzco*, is extensively smoked in many parts of the Andes, much as freebase and crack are smoked elsewhere. At the time they were working Rusby – and Bignon – had found a way to solve the continuing problems of shipping the highly perishable and bulky leaf. Crude cocaine did not deteriorate and it took up far less room, so a far larger quantity could be safely shipped.

For Peru, the vast demand for coca leaf which emerged from 1885 onwards (the year, incidentally, that Coca-Cola was originally formulated) came as manna from heaven. The Peruvian economy had recently suffered from a disastrous war with Chile, but there had been other calamities as well. Coca and cocaine epitomised more than just a lifeline to an ailing country: they came to represent modernity and a golden future. Within five years Peru was exporting huge quantities of leaf, but also a thousand kilos of cocaine sulphate. By 1906 there were nearly two dozen factories producing crude cocaine and the United States was importing well over three-quarters of a million kilos of coca (largely for use in Coca-Cola and other drinks of their ilk) as well as nearly 500 kilos of crude cocaine.

Changing attitudes in the north of Peru would eventually deal a severe blow to the manufacturers of cocaine sulphate but not to the production of the leaf, which still retained a very substantial local chewers market as well. Competition for the leaves for cocaine extraction was already growing, though, but not from sources close by in South America. From the moment cocaine's credentials were first established in the mid-1880s, countries like Britain and Holland, with extensive tropical colonies, sought to find means to transplant the coca plant – much as they had done with other staples of South America, notably quinine and rubber. Coca leaves were delicate; the coca seed was not, and samples were being sent regularly to Kew Gardens in south-west London. From there they found their way to such diverse climates as the foothills of the Himalayas, the Blue Mountains in Jamaica and Lagos in Nigeria. Of these various locations, Assam in India was the most successful and the coca leaf was a successful crop there for many years.

The Dutch, meanwhile, were establishing plantations in Java. As early as 1854 a Dutch botanist called Kasskarl, who had helped set up cinchona (quinine) plantations in India, wrote to the Dutch colonial office to suggest that coca might be equally transportable from South America to south-east Asia. The Dutch government of the time felt, however, that the temptations of coca chewing were such that the natives of Java would succumb to the worst of the excesses described by some of the travellers to Peru.

Whilst initially rejecting the proposal to set up plantations, the Dutch equivalent of Kew Gardens, the Lands Plantentuin based near Jakarta, the modern capital of Indonesia, took coca seeds and planted them in order to evaluate their contents. These seeds developed plants with such a high cocaine content (in some cases double the South American equivalent) that growers throughout Java were invited to try their luck. It was soon found that while much of the local climate was too wet, in higher elevations (the botanic gardens were at 2,600 feet) the coca plants did very well. When the cocaine craze burst upon the world, Dutch growers were well placed to increase production and, by 1889, Java coca leaf was being offered at the recognised international drugs auction rooms (for opium, principally) in Mincing Lane, London.

Despite its high cocaine content, Java leaf suffered from not being South American and therefore not carrying the cachet associated with those leaves. It was also affected by problems associated with the extraction of the cocaine, which was proving to be difficult. The Dutch growers also continued to export the leaves rather than process them into crude cocaine. The breakthrough came when German chemists were able to synthesise the so-called uncrystallisable alkaloid parts of the coca leaf grown in Java. This meant Java leaf could yield up to 2 per cent cocaine, compared with the 0.5 per cent from most South American leaf. Java growers could also count on up to four crops a year. Then, in 1900, the Nederlandsche Cocaine Fabriek (NCF) opened in Amsterdam. By 1910 it had become the largest cocaine manufacturer in the world, producing more than one and a half tonnes of the refined product annually. By this time a cocaine manufacturers' cartel had been set up in Europe, consisting of the eight major European players, who between them agreed not to start any form of price war.

Almost at the same time as NCF became the world's largest maker of cocaine, the first serious doubts about cocaine and its uses began to surface in Europe as well as the United States. For the growers of the leaf this need not have made that much difference, as the demand for coca-containing soft drinks had amply demonstrated the potential demand, if only, at that time, in the United States. But for the manufacturers of cocaine a serious problem of over-supply now threatened. Nothing in contemporary medical literature was available to suggest anything other than that cocaine would become less and less of a requirement. This implied a radical reduction in supply – or a manipulative and increasingly clandestine market for the cocaine not taken up by medicine. The pharmaceutical companies which had so enthusiastically embraced cocaine were now to find themselves dumping it wherever they could.

This problem did not just apply to cocaine. Opium, along with morphine and heroin, was a far greater problem, for growers in this case as well as manufacturers. Even the onset of the First World War, with the resulting desperate need for powerful painkillers, could not swallow up the entire supply of opium. Against the international regulations, nations willing (or, in some cases, reluctant) to sign the Convention were to be set this conundrum; in many cases governments not only turned a blind eye to what was going on, but actively contrived to cook the books.

This became abundantly apparent after the League of Nations took up the mantle of international drug control after the war. The nations which had signed the original Hague Convention had agreed to control the quantities of both raw and refined opium. But none had specified how or, more critically, when. They had further agreed to ensure that no more cocaine, morphine or heroin than was required by medicine would be manufactured. What that amount might be, country by country, had not been specified. The British, with their interests in the opium trade in India and the Far East, were greatly to benefit from this uncertainty. The Dutch, too, with their cocaine factory back home and their burgeoning Java coca plantations were also beneficiaries.

The Dutch had neglected to pass any law demanding returns from Dutch companies about the output of either cocaine or morphine. Even where returns were given – by British companies, for instance – there was no guarantee they were accurate. Examining the records of British exports of morphine to Japan and their records of imports for 1916, the British account shows that 7,257 pounds (3,290 kilogrammes) was exported. However, the Japanese account of imports of morphine from Britain shows more than five times that amount, 37,898 pounds (17,170 kilogrammes). In 1920 only one pound (453 grammes) was apparently exported to Japan by the British, but the Japanese account shows 11,741 pounds (5,320 kilogrammes) arriving. The British Indian government had finally taken over the opium trade by the First World War and the broad view was that the figures they provided were, for this reason alone, bound to be accurate (on the interesting premise that governments do not lie). But in 1918, to take just one year in this period, opium still accounted for 60 per cent of the Straits Settlements' entire revenue.

The League of Nations was to inherit a situation in which the governments who made up its member states, whilst adhering in public to the agreements they had signed on drug control, might well be acting on the ground in an entirely different way. There were very few independent structures in place to counter whatever figures governments decided to supply to the League. On the one hand a number of governments had apparently woken up to the issue of drug-taking on a large scale which, in the British case, they had for well over a century encouraged, at least in others. Some governments, notably Germany and Switzerland, were merely in the business of encouraging their manufacturers to go on making whatever drugs they desired and taxing at least some of the profits. A few governments, like Peru, simply wanted to continue to cash in on what had, after all, been a legitimate source of profit for many years.

The United States was now isolated from Europe and the rest of the world, in part because they did not belong to the League and partly because of the course they followed with regards to alcohol and drugs. As a result, they were officially outside the mess they had helped create. Their crusade, begun before the First World War, had borne some fruit but their main concern in the 1920s was over the extent to which prohibition could be made to work. It was only after it had failed that the United States again became fully engaged with the drugs issue.

After the early Hague Conventions, the British and the Dutch governments both passed Acts which emphasised a medical approach to drugs problems. The Germans were even more circumspect at this time, although, after the Hague Conventions, they did begin to tighten up regulations concerning the wholesale distribution of morphine. In Berlin and Hamburg before 1910, there were any number of morphine 'shops' offering, for example, discounts on second injections of the drug. It was also possible to buy morphine bon-bons and praline sweets.

None of these countries had gone through anything like the cocaine mania of the USA, it has to be said. In all three countries (and in France where the 'drug' problem up until 1914 was absinthe) the number of addicts was limited. Most were victims of careless medical practice and consequently were treated as patients, not as deviants or criminals. In Europe medical practice was long established, whereas in the USA it simply did not carry the requisite clout when it came to federal law-making. As we have seen, the high ground was seized by a curious mixture of religious zealots and professional axe-grinders (like the redoubtable Dr Wiley and his team).

Despite this, the international stage on drugs controls had effectively been set by the United States and although they were not members of the League of Nations, they maintained a presence throughout the 1920s and 1930s. As the twentieth century wore on, the influence of the States would grow to its present universal and highly oppressive level. By the late 1930s, for example, the USA had managed to get marijuana included on the international proscribed list, along with coca leaves. In so doing, as with their own bitter experiences of banning alcohol, they were creating the conditions which would lead decades later to internationally based, highly organised criminal conspiracies in the business of running drugs, not infrequently involving governments and their militaries. In the 1930s, they were already missing the point that it was not the production of opium, coca or marijuana which was the problem, if problem there was. Neither was it, as was played out endlessly in the press (and occasionally on film) a hell-bent set of wily orientals attempting to take over the 'civilised' world through opium dens and cocaine parlours. The problem was the pharmaceutically pure cocaine, morphine and heroin still being manufactured in large quantities, well in excess of anything medicine could possibly need, which made its way onto the official market only to disappear through a combination of ill-kept or deliberately misleading books.

Holland had passed an Opium Act in 1919, an Act which was less a law to prosecute offenders and more a means of administrating the system. There, the biggest scandal which broke between the wars concerned the company Chemische Fabriek Naarden (CFN). In 1928 a box containing 60 kilogrammes of heroin was found in Rotterdam harbour. As a result of further investigations, extensive circumvention of the law was found. CFN had sent the box via the Belgium port of Antwerp on a ship bound for China, calling at Rotterdam. The company was found to have imported and exported huge amounts of the drugs covered by the various Conventions: 950 kilogrammes of morphine, 3,000 kilogrammes of heroin and 90 kilogrammes of cocaine between 1927 and 1928. Despite this, CFN had broken no Dutch law and was not prosecuted. The Naarden case did, however, lead to the League of Nations' Limitation Treaty of 1931. This Treaty attempted to regulate all phases of the production of drugs, from the time the raw materials arrived in a processing plant to the time it was signed off in a hospital, laboratory or druggist's.

While opium was being smuggled into Europe, mainly from Turkey, the cocaine which found its way onto the black market nearly all came from Germany; the large Dutch cocaine plant of Nederlandsche Cocainefabriek, from all that is known, was in the clear. Some of the cocaine which came out of Germany made its way to Britain and thence to the United States. Some was also bound for Japan, which by this time was creating a huge underground market for both opiates and cocaine in the Far East.

The Japanese attitude towards drugs like cocaine and heroin typifies much of what went for official policy at large, excluding the United States, during the period between the Hague Conventions and the end of the Second World War. Put bluntly, as long as the domestic drugs problem was under control, exporting drugs to other countries either as raw material like opium, or as finished product, like cocaine, was not deemed so bad. This had long been the attitude of the British.

Japan was almost drugs free. For instance, they did not have a culture of opium smoking, far from it. The Japanese did sign the Hague Convention of 1912, the Geneva International Opium Convention of 1925 and the Limitation Treaty of 1931, but there were few means available to enforce the regulations from outside any country's borders. Internally Japan had a simple system of controls, not even requiring licensing. Drugs companies did not have to keep any records of their transactions. A further oddity was that where Japan held territories (like Taiwan, which the Japanese had seized in 1895), the few regulations which did apply were only for opium. There was no mention of cocaine, heroin or morphine. Finally, as is still the case, the relationship between commercial entities and the Japanese government was very close and there were many overlaps in personnel. The inter-war period saw the rise of the military in Japan and, as time went on, various parts of that vastly expanding and crucial facet of Japanese life actively engaged in the drugs trade to help finance the wars in which Japan indulged. Drugs money also helped to fund the administration of the huge areas Japan occupied in Manchuria and China. By the end of the Second World War, when all this came to light, the Japanese were found to be running the world's biggest heroin factory – in Manchuria.

With cocaine, the situation was less stark in terms of quantity but no less indicative of what had been going on. After the First World War a few large pharmaceutical companies, all with close ties to the Japanese government of the time, were importing coca leaves from both Java and Taiwan. The processed cocaine was sold to wholesalers, who then divided their product into the decreasing amount required by legitimate sources and the increasing amount re-exported to countries like India (which by this time was reporting a significant cocaine problem). The cocaine which made its way to India kept the brand names it left Japan with – Sankyo, Hoshi, Dai Nippon. Smugglers who obtained their supplies from doctors would invent names, one of the most famous being Fujitsuru, well known in the global underworld of the 1930s.

The great depression of 1930 affected Japan as it affected the rest of the world. Afterwards, only coca leaves from Japanese-owned plantations in Java, or from Taiwan, would be allowed into the mother country for processing. This finally shut the Dutch growers out of the market, but they had already been in trouble since the Dutch adherence to the 1925 Geneva Convention. From the 1930s, Japan was effectively out of control on the international scene although, in an act which might otherwise be seen as breathtakingly cynical, its representatives continued to attend League meetings on drugs controls until 1933. By this time Japan's own accounts of domestic drug production were turning into pure fantasy. After 1933, Japan withdrew entirely from League meetings. Neither cocaine nor heroin production could ever be said to have made a huge impact on the Japanese war chest. Profits from these enterprises were merely incorporated, like most other aspects of the Japanese economy, into the war machine which would lead a nation past the insanely vainglorious attack at Pearl Harbor to the equally (in some views) insane response by the Allies of Hiroshima and Nagasaki.

Finally, in the United States legal cocaine production had fallen off rapidly after the Harrison Act had been passed. Conversely the importation of coca leaf had soared, fuelling the insatiable thirst of good Americans for Coca-Cola. In Europe, the defeat of Germany in 1945 finally put an end to any source of pure cocaine there. The number of addicts in Germany remained higher than anywhere else in Europe. Much of that was the result of proximity to a source of the drug. The Nazis, while publicly condemning drug use, were notoriously afflicted with a craving for cocaine. This might be seen as a parallel both to the decadence of their regime and, once again, to the association of cocaine with a manic excitement. Goering was the most prominent of the senior figures in the regime who used cocaine. There have been some suggestions that Hitler used it as well. Many other senior figures in the Nazi regime have also been implicated in the use of the drug.

The period between the Hague Convention of 1912 and the end of the

Second World War in 1945 is characterised by a shifting of emphasis, fuelled by the United States. All recreational drug-taking or, more specifically, drug-taking outside medical parameters, was perceived to be a threat to the fabric of society. In part, this concept harks back to the old racial stereotypes and to moral panics about the corruption of the young, or about white slavery. In part, drug-taking began to revolve around the entertainment industry which would go through a huge expansion in the second half of the twentieth century. The entertainment industry has always retained a high level of minorities, ethnic or otherwise. These strands would come together with youth culture in an explosive combination, in the baby-boomer years of the 1960s. Cocaine already had a history in the entertainment industry, where its attraction from the start had been that heady mix of expense and excitement.

8

CLEAR AND PRESENT DANGER:
THE ORIGINS OF THE DRUGS WAR

IN THE YEAR 1900 COCAINE was on the cusp between worship and demonisation in the United States. In Europe, its use or abuse had hardly surfaced above the waters of medical practice. In both continents things were about to change. A key element in that change would be the shift in cultural perceptions: whilst nineteenth-century America took nearly all its cultural cues from the Europeans, twentieth-century Europe would slowly but surely begin to take an increasing number of its own from the Americans. Of course, resistance would remain high in places, notably France. But other countries, most obviously Britain, would discover the United States as a source of modernity and excitement. In this, cocaine played an early but critical part.

At the time of the great cocaine craze in America, those in Britain who were interested in any kind of recreational drug use were few. They were almost exclusively to be found among the literary circles of the decadent movement, an extension of interest which can be seen to go back at least as far as Coleridge, de Quincey and the rest. Most within this group who espoused drug use were not thinking of cocaine but the usual suspects: opium (rather than morphine) and hashish (cannabis).

In the 1890s, there was a heady sense of fin de siècle. It was France rather than England or Great Britain in general on which much of this centred; the French 'Club des Hashischins' was one focus, but there were others. Cocaine remained of interest in some literary circles, in part promoted in the public mind by the likes of Dr Conan Doyle and his famous detective. But it is worth noting that Dr Watson was wont to ask whether Holmes was injecting cocaine or morphine. Earlier, Charles Dickens had brought opium smoking into *The Mystery of Edwin Drood* and Oscar Wilde had introduced the same subject into that definitive work of late nineteenth-century decadence, *A Picture of Dorian Gray*.

The various artistic movements of the time were self-conscious expressions of a rejection of base materialism at a time when the empires of Europe were reaching their apotheosis, notably those of Great Britain, France, Holland and Belgium, and to a lesser degree Germany. There were counter-currents which suggested that whilst the glory of empire was an ever-present fact, a great danger lay in the very effete nature of, for example, decadence. This would be reinforced in Britain by the Boer War and would reach its appalling conclusion in the carnage of the First World War. Many people, to begin with, saw the First World War as a necessary sacrifice of young blood, needed to cleanse nations of, for instance, creeds of hedonism and ennui.

Against this view, there had been a considerable and revived interest in Europe in both opium and cannabis as drugs which could be employed outside medicine to alleviate more diffuse conditions. A good general term for these conditions is 'future shock', in particular our old friend neurasthenia. Experiments which, much like Freud's, shaded imperceptibly into simple accounts of self-medication combined with literary descriptions, were conducted by a wide variety of doctors, their acquaintances and others. Havelock Ellis, best known for his work on the psychology of sex (and of homosexuality) tried mescaline (from the mushroom) and wrote about it a good fifty years before Aldous Huxley. Theories about addiction were everywhere, but there was little real understanding of the subject. (Again, a comparison with the United States is useful. The States were at this time on the painful road to an understanding that cocaine could be just as dangerous with regards to addictive qualities as morphine, although the action might be very different.)

There was a great interest in psychological matters at this time, as the entire Freudian movement would rapidly attest, in particular the role of the unconscious. As with the Romantic movement of a century before, it was opium and cannabis (and the rare foray into mescaline) that created the right conditions for these kinds of studies. Cocaine does not fit at all into a mind-numbing, consciousness-expanding model; the opposite is true, in fact. But cannabis at least was also seen more prosaically as a simple remedy for the travails of everyday life.

Walter Ernest Dixon, who was to be a prominent member of the Rolleston

Committee on Morphine and Heroin Addiction in the 1920s (and an opponent of the American model of penalising addicts), looked in detail at how cannabis worked in the 1890s. He took it himself, as well as experimenting on animals (used on ferocious dogs, he found it calmed them down). Dixon's conclusion was this:

> Hemp taken as an inhalation (smoked) may be placed in the same category as coffee, tea and kola. It is not dangerous and its effects are never alarming, and I have come to regard it in this form as a useful and refreshing stimulant and food accessory, and one whose use does not lead to a habit which grows upon its votary.

Hashish and opium use did become fashionable outside the world of art and literature during the 1890s. Then, and also during the Edwardian period, this was fuelled by interest in and around artistic movements. Cocaine was the ghost at this banquet; already it was beginning to find a reputation for unsavoury results. It was, curiously, also seen as an effeminate drug, one which women or the weaker of men would succumb to. It would never lose (even up to the end of the century) its reputation in the world at large as a drug which had a high potential for enslaving women to a life of debauched sex and prostitution.

In Britain, cocaine's first public outing in the new century was to be as the means of final dispatch of the two actresses Edith and Ida Yeoland, briefly mentioned earlier in this book. They committed suicide in July 1901 in Bloomsbury, having obtained the cocaine which killed them by getting their landlady's servant to go and buy it at a local chemist. By this time they would have known, from isolated medical cases, that injecting a large quantity of cocaine would be fatal. Their deaths were remarked upon at the time less for their method of suicide and more for the perils of a life on the stage for certain 'types' of women.

Cocaine's dangers were well recognised. The *Daily Mail* wrote of the deaths of the two sisters:

> The habit grows rapidly; a mild ten per cent solution obtained at a chemist's to cure a toothache has given many people a first taste of the joys and horrors of cocaine. The first effect of a dose is extreme exhilaration and mental brilliancy . . . Yet any chemist will tell you that it has been increasingly in demand by women of late years.

These women, presumably, looked to assuage whatever sorrows they might have had by taking it, much as a later generation of women would be accused of taking too many tranquillisers.

The Yeoland sisters had apparently been heavy users of cocaine: many empty bottles were found at their lodgings. It would explain why they used it to kill themselves. A more usual (and indescribably terrible) means of suicide at that time for women was swallowing carbolic acid. The *Daily Mail* had gone on to suggest that cocaine was in (mis)use among doctors, writers, artists and politicians. Ordinary folk were not included; although the availability of cocaine concoctions from local pharmacies without prescription was widespread, these would have been more expensive than laudanum. In the States cocaine was still in widespread use: a 1903 committee on drug abuse there had declared that cocaine users included 'bohemians, gamblers, prostitutes, night porters, bellboys, burglars, racketeers, pimps and casual labourers'. The panic had already set in. In Britain it would come with the First World War, for not dissimilar reasons.

That 'great' and all-changing war, which began in August 1914, was to shake up more than the political systems in Europe. It heralded the onset of a new world, in which technology would ally itself to killing and in which people would discover new levels of alienation from their fellow beings and from themselves. A desire to escape in any form or fashion from the horrors confronting a soldier minute by minute, hour by hour, was tempered only by the knowledge that the most obvious – running away – was likely to lead to swift and final retribution at the hand of a firing squad. Alcohol would play a huge part in this war in taking the edge of existence off, as it would in all subsequent ones, attested by participants' written and verbal accounts; not, though, by official statistics. Officers, as likely to retreat to the whisky bottle as their men were to the rum, could not discipline their men too far in this regard. Indeed, an issue of rum before men went over the top was in general orders. Tobacco, too, fed a habit at that time uncluttered by any knowledge about long-term health dangers.

As far as other drugs go, availability, as well as facts about their effects, would have been the limiting factor. Later, military commands would self-consciously issue amphetamines – not in production until the 1930s – and later still soldiers themselves would use street wisdom to ensure they had ample supplies of their own preferred drugs (usually cannabis or heroin). Morphine was available in the First World War, but would have been relatively easy to detect among users through their enforced proximity to others and their behaviour. It is interesting to speculate how widespread morphine use by soldiers, especially officers, was during both world wars.

The use of cannabis was probably confined to British Empire troops. To some extent, this also seems to have been the case with cocaine. Canadian soldiers are the prime suspects. But it was perfectly possible to buy small boxes of cocaine powder to snort from many fashionable London stores, including Harrods, during the early part of the First World War. Girlfriends reputedly handed these boxes to their loved ones before they left for the front. One peculiar fact of this war was that it was so physically close to London. Men on leave could catch the cross-channel ferries leaving France and be back in the arms of their loved ones a couple of hours later. The big artillery guns firing across the trenches in northern France could be heard from all over southern Kent.

A cocaine scare finally surfaced with a vengeance in 1916, which also happened to be the worst year of the war so far for Britain, especially after the debacle of the Somme. Significantly, it was women who were blamed. In general the implication was that prostitutes, some of whom were users of cocaine, were drugging the men they went with to rob them and might also be the source of a 'cocaine craze'. The British government had already moved against what Lloyd George had called the deadliest foe (more to be feared than either the Germans or the Austrians): alcohol. There had been a shell scandal in 1915 (far too few reaching the front in France had exploded on being fired). Much of this was traced back to drunkenness in ordnance factories and, as a result, the first public licensing laws were brought in.

Under the Defence of the Realm Act (DORA), many more restrictions to people's daily lives were to follow. Among them was an order preventing people loitering near strategic installations and a 'beauty sleep' order which closed restaurants at 10 p.m., while theatres were forced to finish all performances by 10.30 p.m. Nightclubs were at first exempt from all these rules, but by November 1916 pressure from the press, notably *The Times*, brought them into line, although they were permitted to stay open until midnight at weekends.

This exemption did not last and nightclubs were soon closing at the same time as pubs. Many simply carried on illegally; it is estimated there were as many as 150 operating in this way in Soho alone. With this switch to illegal operations came hints that drug-taking was beginning to become more than a question of quiet middle-class morphine indulgence, or of the odd journey to an East End Chinese den for a spot of opium smoking. London's *Evening Standard* reported:

> West End Bohemia is hearing some dark stories of what is going on. But still more prevalent is the use of that exciting drug cocaine. It is easy to take – just snuffed up the nose; and no one seems to know why the girls who suffer from this body and soul racking habit find the drug so easy to obtain.
>
> In the ladies' cloakroom of a certain establishment two bucketfuls of thrown-away small circular cardboard boxes were discovered by the cleaners the other day – discarded cocaine boxes.

The big scandal broke during 1916 when the use of cocaine among denizens of the demi-monde appeared alarmingly to spill over and directly involve the war effort. In the spring of 1916 the police in London arrested a William Johnson close to Charing Cross, one of the major train terminals taking troops to the front. He had eleven boxes of cocaine in his pocket but protested that he was only trying to sell them to women, adding, in case the police thought he was trying to pick these women up, 'I am only trying to sell cocaine.' The boxes contained a hundred milligrammes each, about a couple of lines or so. He was charging 12.5p a box. Johnson said he had got the cocaine from a local pharmacy, whose owner later admitted in court that he had supplied Johnson with around 150 grammes in all.

Official concern about cocaine had already begun to grow in other places, quite possibly because of the use of it by soldiers (and not just officers). Concern finally settled on Canadian troops stationed in Folkestone, Kent, where they were apparently getting their cocaine locally. One Canadian major believed that at least a few dozen of his men were addicted to it. There had already been more than a hint that the Canadians were bringing their own supply of cocaine from North America. They were well known for insolence and unruliness away from the battlefields, though probably this had more to do with a differing culture than any degree of drug-taking. Whatever the root cause, the implication came to be that there was a market for cocaine among some soldiers and this was being initially supplied through the London outlets.

The existing law, including the mass of wartime regulations brought in with the DORA, did not specifically cover cocaine although those rules relating to the sale of poisons could be, and were, extended to it. During this time both a well-known West End pharmacy, Savory and Moore, and Harrods were prosecuted for selling cocaine and morphine without applying the elementary rules. Both stores had failed to obtain the names and addesses of those to whom they sold their cocaine and there had not been proper prior 'introductions' of the purchasers (by, one presumes, doctors). Savory and Moore had advertised cocaine packets in *The Times*, describing them as 'useful presents for friends at the front'. *The Times*, a little later, would describe cocaine much as Lloyd George had drink, by saying it was a threat to soldiers 'more deadly than bullets'.

The press, ever anxious to make mountains out of molehills and at a time when verifiable news from the Front was almost impossible to obtain, whipped up a storm over this and other transgressions in drug use. As a result the government asked its Select Committee (on the Use of Cocaine in Dentistry) in 1917 to look into what was by then illegal use of cocaine. It concluded: 'There is no evidence of any kind to show that there is any serious, or perhaps, noticeable prevalence of the cocaine habit amongst the civilian or military population of Great Britain.'

The Defence of the Realm Act had in 1916 been amended under Regulation 40B to secure stricter controls on both cocaine and opium smoking. An Army Council order of 11 May, a couple of months before the great Somme offensive, had banned the unauthorised supply to the troops of cocaine, opium, morphine, heroin and cannabis. It was later to become clear that the scare over cocaine and the Canadian troops might have involved as few as a hundred of the quarter million Canadian soldiers who passed in and out of the UK that year.

London's bohemian theatre and clubland scene held on despite the tightening regulations through the latter years of the war. Evidence for that surfaced once more in November 1918 when a popular actress, Billie Carleton, was found dead in bed just after the Armistice. She had attended a victory ball that night at the Royal Albert Hall, Kensington. She had apparently died from an overdose of cocaine, although it is far more likely that she died from barbiturate poisoning. The actress was said to have had a 'frail beauty of that perishable moth-like substance that does not last long in the wear and tear of this rough-and-ready world'. An American club owner in

Soho admitted supplying Billie Carleton with opium. It is easy to imagine any number of recently demobbed military personnel, suffering from the effects of simply surviving the war, adding to the number of casual users of whatever was available.

It was one of Billie Carleton's friends, Reggie De Veulle, who admitted supplying her with cocaine. He stood trial for manslaughter as a result; in the end he was jailed for conspiracy to supply, as the law was still unclear. It would not be clarified until the Dangerous Drugs Act was passed a couple of years later. At the time of the trial, De Veulle's wife admitted to using an opium pipe but not to inhaling, a story that would be used in very different circumstances many years later by a celebrated American and his experience of marijuana.

What this case – and the more notorious one that followed – illustrated was the growing trend among theatrical and now movie types to use cocaine, among other drugs. Lionel Belcher, an actor who worked for the British and Colonial Film Company, along with his girlfriend Olive Richardson, admitted taking cocaine 'absolutely for the fun of the thing', as she put it. The post-war London drug scene remained heavily weighted towards the better middle and upper classes. There is plenty of evidence of opium parties in fashionable apartments and houses, as well as cocaine use. Drug-dealing even took place at the Café Royal in Regent Street. Artists, needless to say, were as much a part of this as always, mixing in with café society. Lady Diana Cooper was used to adding chloroform to morphine by her own admission, and morphine was still the drug of choice among those in the know. There was a continuing emphasis on women using cocaine, one newspaper reporter writing that the most common type of cocaine user was 'young, thin, underdressed, perpetually seized with hysterical laughter, ogling, foolish'.

The Dangerous Drugs Act, passed in 1920, confirmed incidentally that there were three groups taking recreational drugs at this time. First, there were the generally older, often female, morphine users. Next there was a good deal of opium smoking among the Chinese, who bore the brunt of any criminal proceedings. Then there was cocaine, which rapidly became the most used drug. A lot of this had to do with the affectation for all things American which swept through Britain and parts of Europe, a reaction against the European values which had been so comprehensively trashed in the recent war.

In 1922 Freda Kempton, a dance instructress, committed suicide by swallowing cocaine. She had been a heavy user of cocaine and this appears to have kept her sustained in her lifestyle, part of which might well have over-lapped with that of a prostitute. The key difference in her sad story to that of Billie Carelton was the racial element. She had been supplied by a Chinese who went by the name of Brilliant Chang. He was eventually jailed in 1924 for cocaine possession. Chang fitted the stereotype of a foreign corrupter of innocent women. Thus, in Britain the connection was finally made, as it had been in the United States, between drugs, sex and 'lesser' races bent on evil.

The 1920s drugs scene seems to have died down gradually, possibly the result of the dwindling supply of German cocaine from the war. It may finally have been killed off by the Great Depression of the 1930s and a general lack of money, along with the changes in attitude that the Depression brought. Among the rich, drug-taking kept on going at fashionable parties, but cocaine would remain of little interest to drug-takers in Britain until the 1980s. In the United States, too, between 1930 and 1970 cocaine virtually did not figure for users or for the authorities. The authorities, the public, recreational users and addicts simply did not bother much with it; the drugs overwhelmingly in use were marijuana and heroin. Most people who took cocaine were in no way addicts, just users. Those who did occasionally come across cocaine found it 'beautiful . . . but a lot more expensive than heroin'. There were speedballers – those who mixed the cocaine with heroin – but they were few.

Cocaine seizures during this period were tiny. In 1938, after the Marijuana Tax Act had been passed, the United States government seized 558 kilogrammes of bulk marijuana, 18,000 'reefers' (or 'spliffs' to a modern reader) and destroyed 40,000 marijuana plants. The Federal Bureau of Narcotics also seized 674 kilogrammes of opium, 12 kilogrammes of morphine and 94 kilogrammes of heroin, but only 417 *grammes* of cocaine. In the 1940s, '50s and '60s a similar pattern of seizures – with cocaine well down any list – may be discerned. In 1957 Harry Anslinger, head of the Bureau, declared that the United States had no cocaine problem of any kind.

The Federal Bureau of Narcotics (FBN) had been set up in 1930, when the cocaine issue was already dying away in America. The man who ran it for thirty-two years was Harry Anslinger. With Anslinger's appointment the United States had firmly placed its hat in the prohibitive ring, excluding any serious role for medics or academics, for Anslinger's background was diplomacy, not medicine or science. Under his control the FBN, much like J. Edgar Hoover's FBI, took on the mantle of righteous horror still associated with recreational drug-taking in many places. (One only has to look at pronouncements emerging from the British Labour government of Tony Blair in the late 1990s to see this.) At the same time the FBN, along with its immediate predecessor, the Federal Narcotic Control Board, was not infrequently associated with scandals in which agents were shown to have been corrupted by the very trade they were trying to eliminate. In the 1950s and '60s there would come a time when the agency actively conspired with the CIA to help test drugs on unsuspecting citizens in the name of that biggest of all crusades: anti-communism.

In the 1930s, the Federal Bureau of Narcotics' first goal became the banning of marijuana, which was effected by the Marijuana Tax Act of 1937. Once again the race card was played to good effect, as fears over the use of cannabis were greatest in those communities with large immigrant Mexican populations. As with blacks in much earlier generations, Mexicans and, later, other Hispanic immigrants, were used as cheap farm labour. As early as the 1920s horrible crimes were attributed to them, among which was, once again, the rape of white women. Looking at the literature written about marijuana at the time, it is difficult to work out whether there was any contact at all between the authorities and the mythic attributions made by them for this mild narcotic, and those who were using it.

Marijuana's importance in the drugs debate can never be overlooked. Many see its use as the entry point for taking other, much harder drugs, including heroin. The concept of a drugs 'career' is still very much an issue for the twenty-first century. The passage of the Marijuana Tax Act by the USA is important because it placed this relatively easy-to-obtain drug, with its mild effects, in the same class as cocaine and heroin.

But, as with a very large part of what has come to be known as narco-politics, reality has little to do with anything. Race and poverty, however, do. There is a view in some quarters that the racial element in the banning of various drugs – opium, morphine, heroin, marijuana, cocaine – is at best irrelevant, at worst deliberately misleading. But there is simply too much evidence, over too long a period, for it not to have played some part. By the 1980s, as we shall see, a racial element was to become overtly enshrined in American federal law. Class, though of less significance today, has also been a factor. Simply put, when the professional, upper and middle classes had more or less sole access to drugs, the authorities hardly worried the way they would when drug use was seen to have spread in all directions. There was a much stronger medical model in place, too, in terms of any treatment deemed to be required. Recently arrived immigrants and poverty tend to go hand in hand; to inhabit the same ghettoes in towns and cities.

From 1914 until the 1960s, the prohibition model held sway and the only question being asked was how effective the policy was in terms of drugs seizures and drugs-related arrests and convictions. There were sub-plots: as always sections of the middle and even upper classes in the United States would, from time to time, succumb to the temptation of using drugs, often in conjunction with visits to nightclubs. There remained a constant problem for the authorities with the entertainment industry. Black jazz players and singers kept on using marijuana and heroin, sometimes as speedball combinations of the latter with cocaine. Individuals were sometimes caught in the act and punished.

A major geographical problem area was Hollywood, from the first time it was used for making films. Parts of the American film industry in general had always been interested in drug-taking. Hollywood took to cocaine, naturally, and various scandals would break from time to time. One notable early one involved the silent-film star Fatty Arbuckle (who was also supposed to have used a Coca-Cola bottle in a sex act with one of his many women). In the 1920s Cole Porter wrote his famous lyric 'I get no kick from cocaine', later amended to 'I get no kick from champagne', a close enough analogy, all things considered. Tallulah Bankhead, among the many, many Hollywood people who used cocaine, famously remarked to Louise Brooks (of *Lulu* film fame): 'Don't tell me cocaine is habit-forming. I've been taking it for 17 years and I ought to know.' Quite. The fact was – and is – that cocaine was capable of killing those who could not handle it; plenty could, but others, as with today, could not. But the Hollywood and other parties continued. The issue had moved on and cocaine, excluding the huge Asia market and the Japanese connection, slowly sank from general public view. It never went away – no recreational drug ever does.

The portrayal of drugs in movies had been banned under the so-called Hayes Code of 1934 (along with all manner of portrayals of sexual acts and of nudity). There were few exceptions to this. One was a film about the work of the FBN's worldwide efforts to prevent drug-smuggling into the USA (*To the Ends of the Earth*, released in 1948). Robert Mitchum was 'busted' about the same time for possession of marijuana, as other Hollywood stars would be later. In some states by the 1950s the death penalty was introduced for the sale of heroin to minors (in 1956). By the latter half of this decade there was a slow retreat from some of the worst aspects of these policies, with a resultant ever-so-slight trend towards the medical model.

The FBN had a small budget throughout this time; their principal method of attack on drugs use was to demonise them and their effects so completely as to suggest that a single use would lead inevitably to addiction and death. After the Second World War and into the 1950s cocaine was often mixed with heroin, now well-established over its earlier, weaker cousin, morphine. Speedballs were popular, as cocaine itself has always been, with jazz and other pop musicians. Even so, from the 1930s to the 1960s, cocaine went through a period of quiet use; available but expensive and all but forgotten, compared with the frenzy of turn of the century America. The big drug issues of the 1950s and early 1960s concerned heroin and marijuana, as well as amphetamines, which were to make such an impact from the late 1950s on, both in the United States and Europe. But the biggest of changes came not directly from the drug world, or the sub-culture of drug-taking, but from youth culture and the growing financial muscle of the first post-Second World War generation.

The origins of what has been come to known as the 'swinging sixties' began long before, somewhere around the late 1940s and early 1950s. The source was the United States where the post-world war brought a mixture of unparalleled prosperity and with it a huge boom in births (hence the term, baby-boomers). Seventy-five million Americans were born between 1946 and 1957; by 1965 half of America was under 30 years old, coming of age with television and, partly through it, a need for constant gratification. Cocaine played little part in the antics of those most associated with these times; it remained a very minor player and so, it has to be emphasised, did all other drugs, given what was about to take place. To understand what happened from the 1970s right up to the present time, we have to take a look at the huge shift in public perception which took place in the 1960s, much of it around the question of drug-taking and the meaning of personal space and freedom.

This was a period of constant political paranoia about the communist threat, starting more or less as soon as the Second World War had ended and reinforced by the inexorable rise of the atomic and then the hydrogen bombs. In the United States in particular, but spreading to Europe which was now effectively the permanent front line for the Western alliance, there was a constant sense that it might all end tomorrow. This was epitomised by American troops permanently stationed in Europe as part of NATO. The feeling was palpable. The 1960s also saw the assassinaton of President Kennedy – himself a recreational drug user according to at least one accredited source – and the Cuban Missile Crisis. Later, in the United States, there was an explosion of violence over black rights and perhaps most significant of all, the Vietnam War and its effects on young people in America.

It is ironic, then, that the drug which came to symbolise the 1960s – LSD, or acid – should have been developed during the 1950s as a weapon to be used in the Cold War. It was also tested fairly indiscriminately by the CIA, among other US government agencies, on unsuspecting human subjects. In the USA, the military were also gaily spreading 'harmless' bacteria in the New York subway system to observe how a real germ warfare attack might develop.

Acid later came to be experimented with by a generation of Beats, who are important because they espoused a philosophy which would later become an integral part of much of what made the 1960s 'swinging'. The Beats were later dubbed Beatniks, in a side reference to the Soviet Union's sputnik satellites. They were a small group of writers and intellectuals, best characterised by Allen Ginsberg, Jack Kerouac and William Burroughs. Others like Aldous Huxley would also come to be associated with them. Their counter-cultural theme – it never really coalesced into a full-blown set of tenets – was later summed up by Timothy Leary, the ultimate guru of LSD, as: 'Turn on, tune in, drop out.'

A growing assorted group of the rich, the academic and later almost anyone who had anything to do with the entertainment industry would ally themselves at some point to the Beats' themes. The nihilistic nature of their underlying principles, looked at from the viewpoint of the twenty-first century, is now much clearer. These were times which appeared to promise a miraculous future of unprecented wealth and prosperity, whilst simultaneously suggesting both a shallowness of meaning within mere materialism and the likelihood of a horrific end in a nuclear holocaust. Given these circumstances, along with an American way of life which to many seemed as superficial as it was possible to imagine, it is no surprise to find that this group turned to the margins of society to find or create meaning. They turned to black culture and jazz; even criminal activity (Burroughs at one point bought a machine-gun along with a large quantity of morphine); anything, in fact, to escape the mind-deadening daily life that President Eisenhower's 1950s America was shouting from the rooftops.

It is no surprise, either, that in their drug-taking they lighted eventually upon mind-altering drugs, after running through the gamut of marijuana and heroin (cocaine seems not to have figured at all in these forays). The drugs which came to represent the real power of change were the hallucinogenic mushroom derivatives, mescaline and psilocybin and, when it became more readily available, LSD. In their quest for enlightenment, the Beats pushed boundaries beyond reasonable norms. Burroughs, for example, accidently shot and killed his wife after a heavy afternoon's drinking. He later fled to Algiers, a long-time destination of other fugitives from justice or themselves. Here he hit rock bottom, hardly eating, never changing his clothes and sticking a needle into whatever space left on his wrecked body he could find. *Naked Lunch*, his own testament of these times, says much about what happened to him. Meanwhile Jack Kerouac took to the (American) road, out of which has come one of the greatest single paeons to Beat lifestyle and self-discovery, *On the Road*.

Ginsberg, like Burroughs but with seemingly more conscious purpose, shovelled every drug he could get his hands on into his body by one route or another. He was not, however, a heroin addict, as he claimed for a long while. Most of the Beats stuck with marijuana, as it happened, although heroin use was prevalent too. But marijuana was beginning to escape all ghettoes, poor and intellectual. Both simultaneously fascinated and horrified by the antics of the Beats, middle America, and especially young white students, were slowly taking their first steps towards the explosive use of the drug which would become part of the true picture of the 1960s. (LSD was wildly publicised but never achieved anything like the same casual levels of use as marijuana.)

It was in 1960 that Ginsberg first met Timothy Leary, a Harvard-trained clinical psychologist. Leary's wife had recently committed suicide and after a period in Europe drifting around, Leary had returned to the United States to work. Then, in 1960, he had gone on holiday to Mexico where he tried psilocybin (magic mushrooms). This event was utterly to change his life. A flavour of what happened may be garnered from one of his books: 'Listen! Wake up! You are God! You have the divine plan engraved in cellular script within you. Listen! Take the sacrament! You'll see! You'll get the revelations! It will change your life! You'll be reborn!'

Leary never deviated from his views about hallucinogens. In 1960 he came home to set up an ambitious research programmeme, obtaining supplies of psilocybin from Sandoz, who also made LSD. There are many parallels here with Sigmund Freud 80 years earlier and the German firm of Merck (Sandoz had Swiss origins). LSD, like cocaine in the 1880s, was still legal. Freud had perceived the future of cocaine as a cure-all, largely for physical health. In the psychologically obsessed twentieth century (which owed a lot to Freud's own swerve of career after his possibly cocaine-induced paranoid panic over what he had done) LSD came, albeit briefly, like cocaine to represent the drug which would liberate humankind from its everyday existence, which Freud himself had memorably called 'an island of pain in a sea of misery'.

Lysergic Acid Diethylamide-25 had first been isolated from the fungus ergot in 1942. Ergot was the same rye fungus which had driven peasants from the Middle Ages into well-documented frenzies of odd behaviour. Albert Hofmann, the research director of Sandoz at that time, found out what LSD could do when he accidently swallowed some. When he tried it again under more scientific conditions, one of the feelings he described as having was 'as if I were out of my body'. He believed, given the range of other effects it created, that it could usefully be applied to psychiatry. But there was a war on and the progenitor of the CIA, the OSS, had been set up. This clandestine organisation had already tried using cocaine, marijuana, heroin, morphine, ether, benzedrine, alcohol and even ether on prisoners, who knew nothing of what was going on, and on their own volunteers. Nothing had looked particularly promising.

After the war, once investigated a little, LSD looked like an entirely different proposition. From the 1950s, now locked into the Cold War, the new agency of the United States' clandestine policies, the CIA, began to undertake an amazing array of 'experiments' to see if this drug could be used to interrogate prisoners, debrief spies or wreak havoc on the enemy. In one test black prisoners, held on drugs charges, were given LSD for over two months continuously, the dosage rate sometimes being up to quadruple that which was considered to be normal. There was a high expectation that this would create insanity among some of those experimented on. This all took place at a government prison ostensibly created to 'cure' drug abuse.

In 1953 the Director of the CIA, Allen Dulles, authorised a top-secret programme of LSD testing on federal prisoners, foreigners, mentally ill patients and the terminally ill, designed to see how much use the drug could be to the American government. CIA agents also tested LSD on each other, sometimes spiking the morning coffee of a colleague and then awaiting the result. At least one of the agents became psychotic after such spiking;

eventually, he killed himself. In another such experiment prostitutes in San Francisco were paid to give clients LSD, as well as take it themselves. Both parties were then secretly filmed to study their reactions.

All this was done with the blessing of that mighty warrior against illegal drugs, the head of the FBN, Harry Anslinger. One of Anslinger's agents, George White, was in charge and he made comments in his reports like 'Gloria gets the horrors, Janet gets sky high'. When White retired he wrote to an old CIA colleague: 'I was a very minor missionary . . . but I toiled wholeheartedly in the vineyards because it was fun, fun, fun. Where else could a red-blooded American boy lie, kill, cheat, steal, rape, and pillage with the sanction and blessing of the All-Highest?'

California became the centre for LSD research and many people outside both the government laboratories and academic establishments testing it willingly tried it. Doctors were officially experimenting with it, too. One, Dr Humphry Osmond, originally from England, gave it to Henry Luce, then head of *Time* magazine and his wife Clare Boothe Luce, then US ambassador to Italy. The writer Anäis Nin also tried it, as did Cary Grant, who by some accounts became a life-long user. By 1965, it has been estimated that between 30,000 and 40,000 psychiatric patients around the world had received it; 2,000 papers on its effects had been published.

Leary first came across LSD in 1961; after initial misgivings, he tried it. Before he took LSD Leary, experimenting with both psilocybin and mescaline, had been anxious to keep science to the fore. After his LSD experience he said to a friend: 'We're through playing the science game.' LSD is a much more powerful drug than those he had been taking before; a comparison between the coca leaf and cocaine comes to mind. The genie was now well and truly out of the bottle and LSD's use and reputation spread outwards and onwards through the campuses of the United States and far beyond. Harvard University sacked Leary in 1963 after a series of incidents surrounding his 'research'. Four years later LSD was available just about anywhere; the summer of love was well and truly making its mark. Now more generally called acid, LSD created its own sub-culture of music, fashion and an attitude, not excluding Leary's 'turn on' credos, of living for 'sex, drugs and rock 'n' roll'.

Those working at the FBN were taken aback by the changes they saw everywhere around them. Anslinger, who retired in 1962, was later to confess his almost complete mystification over these changes. Others in drugs enforcement would find that now, far from being perceived as heroic front-line defenders of the American Way, they were vilified for arresting college kids on possession and dealing charges, almost always for marijuana. To put the change in perspective, in 1965 there were 18,000 state level arrests for possession of this drug. In 1970 there were 188,000. A national survey of 1971 estimated that 24 million Americans over the age of 11 (about 10 per cent of the entire population) had tried marijuana at least once. The number of heroin users had risen from 50,000 in 1960 to half a million in 1970. Some of that could be attributed to what was going on in south-east Asia.

While middle-class American youth was rocking and rolling across the States singing of love and peace, a darker American dream, one which would soon turn into a nightmare, was acting out an unlooked-for role in Asia. By 1967 the United States was locked into an impossible war in Vietnam, one which it would eventually lose. The gradual sucking in first of American 'advisers', then American soldiers, into what was essentially a civil war was first and foremost part of the global perception of the state of the Cold War. By then this was a frozen set of opposing values which seemed still to promise a quick and brutal end to everything.

America had entered the 1960s by electing John Kennedy, a young Catholic president who symbolised hope over despair, action over inertia. It was this over-optimistic sense of almost-divine mission, combined with inexperience and a venality even modern presidents have found it hard to match, which led to the Cuban Crisis of 1962. After that the United States was determined not to let go of what it saw as its advantage over the Soviet Union. Already committed to the domino theory (if one nation fell to the communists, the next would surely follow), the United States determined it must not lose South Vietnam to the North. There was, too, the brooding menace of the communist Chinese. Military strategists fatefully cast their minds back to Korea, where Chinese intervention had nearly lost them the entire venture and had brought them close to using atomic weapons.

By 1967 the United States was committing ever-larger numbers of American soldiers to an impossible conflict. Many were able to dodge the draft (middle-class white kids, in the main). For the mish-mash of poor white and mostly black troops who found themselves stuck in muddy ditches in a country they neither understood nor cared in the slightest for, drug-taking was one way of alleviating the daily horror. Amphetamines, long an official favourite with the military to boost flagging morale for an attack or to keep up spirits on a patrol, were not what the Vietnamese volunteers wanted. They chose the tranquillity of marijuana and heroin. So whilst back home a new and enlarging group of people were tuning in and turning on, thousands of miles away another group, this time with guns and a hardening attitude, were getting as mad as hell while trying to create some form of psychological survival by doing drugs. The eventual coming together of these two disparate groups would seed America's great drugs crisis of the 1970s and 1980s.

Much of the heroin the soldiers in Vietnam were using was being supplied through CIA-backed warlords in countries like Laos; thus do the gods conspire to drive us mad.

In Europe, drug-taking very much followed the US model with a shorter than usual time-lag. Marijuana smoking increased exponentially in the mid- to late-1960s, much of it fuelled by pop-star use. LSD came too, but in nothing like the same amounts. Heroin started to become a problem in Britain when the law changed in 1967, in effect preventing those addicts there were from getting it through prescription from doctors. The Dangerous Drugs Act was passed in theory to reduce the over-prescribing of heroin to addicts who were also obtaining cocaine from a very few London doctors and selling it on. Or so it was claimed at the time by an Interdepartmental Committee on Drug Addiction in 1965. Prescribing cocaine to addicts was more or less a non-issue by 1969. An attempt to look at marijuana more rationally, the Wootton Committee of 1967, came down in favour of decriminalising it, but the Labour government of that time turned the suggestion down. As was happening in the United States, panic would prevail over debate; punishment over either a permissive looking-the-other-way approach or treatment.

Cocaine use in Britain was such a minor issue that it had mostly been forgotten; as with the States, that was to change dramatically in the three decades that followed.

9

THE RETURN OF THE 'CHAMPAGNE' DRUG

IN 1968 THE AMERICAN PRESIDENT most associated with a sustained attack on drugs use was elected: Richard Nixon. Swept in on a general law and order ticket, he wasted no time in setting out an agenda designed to end any form of drugs use in the United States. With Nixon's arrival in the White House the drugs laws period moved decisively into drugs wars. From the beginning of his presidency in 1969 Nixon declared abuse of drugs to be a 'national threat', using long-term associations between drugs use and crime to raise public fears and to galvanise Americans into action. At the same time he pushed Congress to pass new laws, asked for and got a huge increase in funding for anti-drugs campaigns, and expanded the FBN.

The key to Nixon's campaign was his insistence that drugs and crime were synonymous. During the presidential campaign there had been an big growth in crime, along with many urban riots across the country, as well as the assassinations of figures like Martin Luther King and Bobby Kennedy. The United States was still heavily engaged in Vietnam. Many voters saw an association between the failures of the military there and the apparently dissolute and anarchic behaviour of young people at home, for whom casual drug use was seen as part of everyday life.

In July 1969, Nixon told the nation:

> Within the last decade, the abuse of drugs has grown from essentially a local police problem into a serious national threat to the personal health and safety of millions of Americans. A national awareness of the gravity of the situation is needed; a new urgency and concerted national policy are needed at the federal level to begin

to cope with this growing menace to the general welfare of the United States.

Two years later in 1971 he was to add: 'Drugs traffic is public enemy number one domestically in the United States today and we must wage a total offensive, worldwide, nationwide, government-wide, and, if I may say so, media-wide.' These words were backed by a completely false statement that heroin addiction had increased ten-fold between 1969 and 1971.

Back in 1969, the Vietnam War was reaching its crescendo of disarray after the Tet Offensive of the year before. The expected student revolutions of Europe were collapsing and the Summer of Love was looking like a long-lost dream. These disparate events are mixed up with what was about to happen as cocaine went into a feverish revival, seemingly out of nowhere. The Tet Offensive was the turning point in America's direct military involvement in south-east Asia, as it proved that the poverty-stricken peasants of North Vietnam and their southern counterparts could take on and defeat the world's greatest military power with an impudence that took the breath away. Hundreds of thousands of returning GIs, up to 25 per cent of whom had used heroin let alone the countless number who were casual users of marijuana, would be importing their habit back home, hardly in a mood to give it up.

In Europe the disillusionment with radical politics, always mixed in with the hippy element to whom drug use was so natural as to be not worth talking about, would create a generation to whom drugs were not so much of a problem as a simply made choice: about as hard to decide about as whether to have that first cigarette or pint of beer. As with the United States, drug use would increase but remain a minority activity. Many young people did not start using drugs during or after the 1960s in either continent; but many more than otherwise might have been expected to did. The continuing expansion of pop music had something to do with this, as well as other cultural changes. The hype and high-rolling lifestyle of many young rich and working-class musicians would make drugs look cool, as would their admissions that they had used them.

They were about to be assisted in their choices by the interest now taken in drugs by another great entertainment industry: films. In 1969 *Easy Rider* was released. It opened with a serious drugs deal; the drug being traded was cocaine. It is a measure of the innocence of many audiences who first saw *Easy*

Rider that this opening sequence was of far less consequence than those later scenes involving marijuana and then LSD – or the bloody ending which really got everyone talking.

At this time cocaine was poised to make a return. As the drug of choice for many it is still with us, and this time it is unlikely that it will go away. Along with the other major illegal drugs taken recreationally, cocaine's revival as a drug of choice came about through a mixture of factors. But for more than a decade it retained its earlier image as a drug which could be taken with impunity. As with the cocaine fever of the 1880s and 1890s, there has been a price to be paid.

Why did cocaine make a comeback when it did? The principal reason was probably the growing reputation as a killer drug of the mass of amphetamines flooding the legal and black market in the 1960s. Two hundred million tablets of these drugs had been given to American troops in the Second World War. Lovers of British war films will well remember Jack Hawkins, on the bridge of a frigate hunting a U-boat, being fed them by the ship's doctor to keep him awake. After the war they were a popular dance drug. Purple hearts were just one type well used in Britain in the early 1960s. These pills would, in the 1980s, be rapidly replaced by ecstasy as rave parties swept Britain.

In the USA housewives were prescribed amphetamines in tens of millions for depression (the 'mother's little helper' of the Rolling Stones song). The children of these women, growing to teen-age in the 1960s and looking for as many drug experiences as possible, raided their parents' bathroom cabinets to see what they coud find. There was a problem, though, as possibly the most effective anti-drugs slogan in history starkly pointed out: 'Speed kills.' Ironically this slogan has now been expropriated by the police and local authorities in Britain, in an attempt to slow down car drivers. Like much drug argot, its origins have now been forgotten. People talk about getting 'high' on all kinds of things; or of headache pills, once working, as 'kicking in'. They ask if a problem has 'been sorted'. It merely illustrates the point that drugs are everywhere and anywhere and, to tell the truth, we no longer notice that much.

The original 'Speed kills' slogan was aimed at the young, who were literally killing themselves by taking too many uppers. Autopsies were revealing that the young – sometimes very young – bodies of girls and boys had internal organs that looked as if they belonged to the victims' grandparents. Given the plain truth that folk will not stop taking drugs, merely seek different ones, cocaine was an obvious candidate. This was not least because it could be sniffed. Smoking tobacco, although still a highly popular thing to do in the late 1960s, was just beginning to get a bad press. Injecting – as with heroin – was awkward, messy and often all too obvious to others. It was also correctly perceived by many as being very dangerous.

Cocaine was extremely expensive at this time as supplies were scarce, but for the growing affluent society the United States had become by the late 1960s this was a bonus. If you could afford to take cocaine you were making a social statement as well as a recreational choice. There were other factors, too, which helped the cocaine revival along. Nixon's war on drugs began with the one that most people took – marijuana. Uncovering truck-loads of it was relatively easy, as it was bulky and its smell carried to even the most indolent of sniffer dogs. As the supply chain began to be hit the bigger illegal producer players rethought their strategy.

Opium and heroin were not popular for the same old reasons but cocaine, already legally grown as coca plants in very large quantities to the south of the United States, was an obvious option. The coca crops were soon to be diverted into laboratories springing up in the jungles of Peru and Bolivia and, eventually, Colombia. A huge additional advantage was that cocaine was vastly more profitable than marijuana, and furthermore much more easily transported. Although cocaine may well have made its comeback without any assistance, it can safely be said that Nixon's declaration of war on marijuana definitely hastened its revival.

Having tried marijuana and found it pleasurable, the baby-boomer generation leaving US universities in the late 1960s and early 1970s were likely to try other drugs that offered even bigger doses of pure pleasure. As news spread, cocaine's ability to make people feel immensely good very quickly, allied to its initial implied charge of increased sexuality, ensured it would become the drug of choice for a growing number. Even at universities its use increased – ten-fold on some campuses – between 1970 and 1980. One commentator pointed out it was everywhere in New York by the mid-1970s and that people, far from hiding their use, would snort it openly. Cocaine use had become chic.

More films were contributing to the general view that this drug, at least, was super-cool. In Woody Allen's *Annie Hall*, audiences, some more knowing than others, laughed loudly when Allen's own character managed to sneeze thousands of dollars' worth of cocaine when shown a box of it by a friend. All the characters in the film are rising middle-class professionals. In *Superfly*, blacks are shown dealing in it; moral judgements in all these cases were suspended, not present at all, or implied that this was fine, this was OK.

In 1971 *Newsweek*'s life and leisure section had called cocaine 'the status symbol of the American middle-class pothead'. There were quotes in newspapers and magazines suggesting that orgasms were better when cocaine was used, and the deputy director of Chicago's Bureau of Narcotics suggested that 'you get a good high with coke and you don't get hooked'. The flood of articles continued, many referring back to the cocaine fever of the previous century. In 1974 the *New York Times* magazine, in an uncanny repeat of the *New York Times* leader of 1885, headlined an article: 'cocaine: the champagne of drugs', suggesting in the article that 'for its devotees, cocaine epitomises the best of drug culture – which is to say, a good high achieved without the forbiddingly dangerous needle'.

Many other newspaper articles mentioned the patent medicine boom, where cocaine had been used; even more took delight in recalling the battles between the various colas of that time, including Coca-Cola. Few, if any, of these articles or the many other mentions of cocaine, discussed the addiction problems which had developed, nor the sexual dysfunction that prolonged use in many cases produces. As before, parts of professional America had fallen in love with cocaine and this time around there was an immense self-hyping publicity machine in the modern mass media, including film and television. By the mid-1970s the media had any number of employees who were regular users of the drug.

It was also highly popular among better-off professionals like lawyers and, of course, doctors, a number of whom were confirming in learned journals as well as to anyone who would listen that cocaine was in no way a problem. Books were beginning to be published which emphasised the same thing. As to why the drug had been banned before, a number of those writing and talking about it at this time lighted upon the race question. Richard Ashley, in his book *Cocaine: Its History, Uses and Effects* (published in 1975), said that cocaine had not been banned because of its long-term addictive qualities (whatever addictive might mean) but because of the increasing use of the drug by blacks and the fears of white society.

In a book by a Harvard Medical School psychiatrist Lester Grinspoon, and co-author James Bakalar, published in 1976 at the height of the new cocaine boom, both writers expressed scepticism over the researches done on cocaine in the earlier period. They went on to say: 'The most significant sociological fact about cocaine today is that it is rapidly attaining unofficial respectability in the same way as marijuana in the 1960s. It is accepted as a relatively innocuous stimulant, casually used by those who can afford it to brighten the day or the evening.' A New York psychiatrist of the time said 'it is rare to find people who use it in large quantities continuously'. The medical view was split, but there were many within the profession in the United States who tended towards the opinion that snorting cocaine two or three times a week (the actual quantities suggest a maximum use of one to two grammes) would create no lasting problem. That is, assuming the sniffer could afford the still-expensive drug in the first place.

By now it was possible to buy all kinds of cocaine-users accessories. A San Francisco jewellery store was offering diamond-encrusted razor blades (to cut the cocaine) at $500 and cocaine spoons for up to $5,000. Suited Wall Street lawyers were spotted at parties with 14-carat gold spoons, although it is quite possible they were using these accoutrements as an indication of their cool as much as actually indulging in any drug-taking. This whole cocaine scene was soon to come to Britain and is still with us. One of the abiding images of 1980s Thatcherite Britain is that of city slickers rushing to the lavatories during the course of their hectic dealing days to snort a few lines, before returning to the hurly-burly to do ever more amazing deals.

Cocaine use had now crossed all kinds of boundaries. By their own admissions, many pop stars of the ilk of Elton John were using huge quantities and, in his case, becoming heavily dependent. It was during this time that Sting would memorably describe cocaine as 'God's way of saying you have too much money.' Many Hollywood stars admitted to taking it, as did others employed in the film industry. One film producer said: 'It's the '70s drug . . . Coke is really easy. Of course you have the occasional lost weekend when you do maybe a gramme or two . . . But it's a neat drug – makes you feel good, you can function on it . . . It's getting bigger all the time'.

It certainly was. By the mid-1970s there was a moment when cocaine just might have become a legal drug again in the United States, along with marijuana. The origins of this quite extraordinary moment in American drugs history are to be found in the establishment of a lobbying group called the National Organisation to Reform Marijuana Laws (NORML) in 1971. Also set up, in 1972, was an organisation called the Drug Abuse Council (DAC), backed by the Ford Foundation, Carnegie, Equitable Life Assurance and others. In a report it published in 1980 the DAC said, *inter alia*: 'Medical experts generally agree that cocaine produces few observable health consequences in its users. In this respect American cocaine use appears to resemble a common pattern in alcohol use in which fine wines or liquors are reserved for other than ordinary consumption.'

Guided by the kind of information emanating from the DAC, a US government White Paper of 1975 argued: 'The data indicates that cocaine is used for the most part on an occasional basis (several times a month or less); usually in the company of others; and it is likely to be taken in combination with alcohol or marijuana, or some other drug. Cocaine is not physically addictive . . . as currently used, usually does not result in serious social consequences such as crime, hospital emergency room admission, or death.' The White Paper did acknowledge there were occasions when cocaine use was of concern but the overall message was that it was not a drug worth worrying too much about.

Perhaps the most startling example of what was happening in the way attitudes had been changing came at the 1981 Academy Awards, compered by America's great chat-show host Johnny Carson, when he joked to his audience: 'The biggest money-maker in Hollywood last year was Colombia. Not the studio, the country.'

By 1981, as it happened, the high-tide of middle-American opinion on drug use had changed. By this date, too, freebase cocaine was becoming much more prevalent: smoking cocaine to increase its effects began among the same people who were snorting it. And, very quickly, an even cheaper method of smoking cocaine would emerge, and the crack cocaine epidemic which swept America in the mid-1980s would begin.

But lest it be forgotten, the 1970s were, with the exception of the start of the President Carter period of office, a time when the war on drugs had been continually stepped up. Cocaine was marginally exempt from some of the efforts put in by federal agencies, largely because its use was confined to professionals – once more the 'problem' of middle-class drug use was sidelined. Nixon's original declaration of war on drugs was never to be rescinded in any way. Out of it would come a huge expansion in the number of people involved: a 'narco-complex' was in the process of being set up from 1969 on; it is still expanding.

The first concrete result of Nixon's rhetoric was the Comprehensive Drug

Abuse Prevention and Control Act of 1971. Perhaps the harshest provision under this law was that which allowed 'no-knock' warrants to be issued by judges. These gave federal agents the right to break into homes or any premises to undertake drugs searches. A great deal of money was also put up for drugs enforcement; the anti-drugs budget climbed from $43 million in 1970 to $321 million in 1975. A huge bureaucracy was beginning to emerge behind all this. Even in the late 1960s the FBN had a budget of only $6 million and a staff of about 300 agents, more or less the number it had been started with in 1932.

A second agency, the Bureau of Drug Abuse Control, had been created in the Department of Health, Education and Welfare in 1965 to regulate hypnotics. In 1968, just before the Nixon years, the Bureau of Narcotics and Dangerous Drugs (BNDD) was created inside the Justice Department – further evidence, if any were needed, that the drugs issue would remain a criminal, not a health question. Then, in 1973, a new super drugs enforcement agency was created out of all the existing ones: the Drugs Enforcement Administration (DEA). In September 1973, Nixon had announced 'we have turned the corner on drug addiction in the United States'. Cynics suggested he said this because he had just won the 1972 election; but the result was that the federal drugs effort was for a time reduced and many parts of its previous programme moved back to state level. Even so, despite Nixon's pronouncement, budgets did not fall off and the DEA continued to expand.

While Nixon's attention had been on the drugs question he had acted to step up treatment programmes at home, particularly methadone regimes for heroin addicts. He had also moved into the international arena to stop supplies reaching the United States. Targeting Turkey on the heroin front, he was largely successful in at least getting the Turkish government to comply with America's dictats (by threatening to cut off aid if they did not). But the Turkish supplies were easily filled by those coming out of Mexico, Afghanistan, Pakistan and the golden triangle of south-east Asia. In the latter case, the CIA were to be indirectly implicated.

The early 1970s saw a huge expansion in addiction treatment: federally funded city programmes meant an increase in those addicts receiving help, rising from 20,000 in October 1971 to 60,000 by December 1972. Most of the treatment aimed to get addicts off heroin by switching them onto methadone. (This method remains highly controversial to this day, as many believe dependence is merely switched from one opiate to another.

Methadone is also thought by some to be the more dangerous; it can take five weeks to get off methadone, against five days for heroin.)

Meanwhile, given the continuing rise in drug use, more novel approaches to drugs use were beginning to emerge. The Commission on Marijuana and Drug Abuse (NCMDA) was set up in 1972 to look first at the widespread use of marijuana and then, within two years, to report back on drug use in general. The Commission comprised mainly traditionally minded members, yet its first report concluded that possession of small amounts of marijuana should be decriminalised. By this they meant that although the law banning it ought not to be repealed, anyone caught with a quantity deemed to be for personal use only would be fined rather than face a prison sentence. The illogicality of a recommendation like this, which entirely begs the question of who is doing the original supplying of the personal quantities of this or any other drug, bedevils this seemingly sensible suggestion whenever it is raised.

The American public found this recommendation hard to swallow as well. Nixon simply refused at all to accept the report he was given in public from the Commission chairman, Pennsylvania Governor Raymond Shafer. The final report came out in March 1973. It reconfirmed the Commission's first thoughts on marijuana while suggesting that all drugs-related issues – enforcement, research, treatment – should be taken care of by a single agency. The final report also recommended that there should be a moratorium on drug education, as the programmes then running were frequently in conflict with each other. Finally, the report pointed out that both alcohol and tobacco remained bigger problems than all the other drugs combined.

A single federal agency, as suggested by the Commission, was not on the cards. Instead many government prevention programmes were brought under the wing of the National Institute on Drug abuse (NIDA), set up in the same year as the Commission report, 1973. NIDA became the focus for drug use research. The demise of President Nixon after the Watergate scandal and the induction of his vice-president, Gerald Ford, signalled a change in drug policies after 1974 which would last well into the Carter years. Ford's attitude, possibly reinforced by his own wife's addiction to alcohol, was that drug use was not going to go away and that any hope of eliminating drug-taking therefore was a pipe-dream.

Recognition of this would come in the United States' *White Paper on Drug Abuse*, published in September 1975. It reviewed efforts going back to 1969 – and implicitly attacked the Nixon policies. It drew the following conclusion:

'Total elimination of drug abuse is unlikely, but governmental actions can contain the problem and limit its adverse effects.' The White Paper also ranked drugs, pointing out that each had its own problems. It said that the main effort needed to be directed against amphetamines and heroin. Neither cocaine nor marijuana were mentioned in the summary of 77 recommendations, despite the Congress of five years earlier insisting that the highest priority be given to marijuana by the Commission on Marijuana and Drug Abuse. The activities of the Commission had also coincided with a massive increase in cocaine use. It was cocaine, and its use by White House staff, which helped lead to a backlash to drugs use among the young by the end of the Carter term of office. In 1977, before this backlash took place, President Carter had asked Congress to abolish all federal criminal penalties for anyone caught with less than an ounce (28 grammes) of marijuana. Although he emphasised that he did not approve of drug use, he pointed out that huge (he actually said most, when the figure at that time was just under 60 per cent) numbers of young people were using marijuana or had used it.

President Carter was a Washington outsider. His single term of office at the end of the 1970s was to be followed by twelve years of single-minded drugs wars, carried on in turn by Presidents Reagan and Bush (the elder). Carter made an effort not merely to turn the debate on drugs in a different direction, but also to make a change in the law. In August 1977, he said: 'My goals are to discourage all drug abuse in America – and also to discourage the excessive use of alcohol and tobacco – and to reduce to a minimum the harm drug abuse causes when it does occur.'

One of his key appointments when he had been Governor of Georgia had been that of British-born psychiatrist Dr Peter Bourne to advise and head up the state's drug programme. Bourne had been head of Georgia's drugs policy in 1971 when Carter was governor. He took a liberal attitude to drugs, which was just as well given that one of Carter's sons had been thrown out of the US Navy for smoking pot. He had also been a major player in Carter's presidential campaign and, once in the White House, Carter made him Special Assistant for Health Issues to the President. Bourne's official attitude was that drugs policy ought to be realistic. He had also written: 'Cocaine . . . is probably the most benign of illicit drugs currently in widespread use. At least as strong a case could be made for legalising it as for legalising marijuana. Short-acting – about fifteen minutes – not physically addicting.' Bourne set about changing federal drugs policy and his personal closeness to

Carter made him highly influential, giving him possibly the greatest power ever for anyone connected with drugs policy in the United States.

Two months after Carter had been inaugurated, Bourne and other officials from the DEA, State Department, the National Institute for Mental Health (NIMH), the NIDA, the Justice Department and the Customs Service went before a House Select Committee on Narcotics Abuse and Control to make the case for decriminalising marijuana. Bourne pointed out that at that time federal law was rarely enforced when it was a question of just possession. In fact, the state of Oregon had decriminalised marijuana in 1973 and Bourne pointed out that no dire consequences had followed. He added that they could not contemplate legalisation because that would violate the United Nations' 1961 Single Convention, which the United States had signed, but lessening the effect of the law would be both permissable and sensible. Five months after this, Carter said that 'penalties against possession of a drug should not be more damaging to an individual than the use of the drug itself; and where they are, they should be changed. Nowhere is this more clear than in the laws against possession of marijuana in private for personal use.'

The efforts of both men, and others, to alter policies on drug use which had been in place for 60 years were about to be destroyed by a series of events – some involving a bizarre twist. What happened highlights an overriding problem, existing across the globe, when it comes to drugs use and policies designed to eliminate supply and demand. It is extremely difficult to separate one drug from another because of the way the laws have been framed; and it is practically impossible to deal with drugs issues on a domestic basis given the global dimensions involved.

While Carter and Bourne were making the case for lightening the laws on marijuana inside America, they also made the case for moving towards entirely eliminating other drugs, notably heroin. As part of the administration's policy in this regard, they supplied the Mexican authorities with money to spray the illegal poppy fields there with herbicides. For the Mexicans, though, the priority was not heroin, but eradicating marijuana which in their eyes was the biggest domestic drugs problem. They began to spray marijuana fields with paraquat. As the news that this was happening spread, so did fears among American users of marijuana that paraquat-laced dope was getting into the lungs of millions and doing untold harm. The American National Association for the Reform of Marijuana Laws (NORML) seized upon this issue to imply that the Carter government was being two-faced in its suggestion of decriminalisation; in fact, it was poisoning the very people it claimed to be supporting. Whilst there was never a single proven case of a paraquat-marijuana smoker being harmed, the Health and Welfare Department issued a press release in early 1978 saying that were a marijuana user to smoke three to five contaminated joints a day for several months, irreversible lung damage would result. After this *faux pas* NORML was determined to nobble Peter Bourne, now demonised as well as being thought two-faced. Its chance came twice: in the false prescription issue and in the allegation that he had snorted cocaine.

Dr Bourne's downfall came because, in the climate then generally abroad in the higher reaches of government, many felt able to pursue their own lives without reference to those laws they did not necessarily agree with. In this regard Bourne wrote a prescription for Quaaludes for his White House assistant Ellen Metsky, under a false name. Unfortunately for them both, a routine check at the chemist shop where she tried to get the drug led directly back to the White House and Bourne. His explanation got him deeper into hot water (he said the false name was to spare her embarrassment, but Quaaludes were well known as a recreational drug).

This incident gave his enemies in NORML, especially its founder Keith Stoup, the opening they needed. Stoup followed the Quaaludes story with one of his own: that Dr Bourne had been seen at a NORML party for 600 people snorting cocaine in a bedroom, where many other people had been present. Dr Bourne has always denied he did anything of the sort. Despite this, in the immediate aftermath, which included his resignation, any chance that marijuana, let alone cocaine, might be legalised or decriminalised in any way disappeared in a puff of smoke. Even so, in 1980 it would still be true to say that whilst Americans knew that cocaine use was spreading, the prevailing view was that sniffing it was neither addictive nor problematic, the majority of users being affluent, white and successful.

The demise of Dr Bourne more or less coincided with the growing backlash in the American public's mind about drugs in general. There had been many worries about the way in which 'the kids' had stopped being interested in activites as mundane but very American as local baseball teams. Parents, one by one, little by little, had become much more conscious of the degree to which marijuana smoking had pervaded their homes. In 1978, the critical year for this change of perception, a housewife called Joyce Nalepka went to a rock concert with her two children and was horrified over the amount of overt drug-taking she saw. She later became president of the National Federation of Parents for Drug-Free Youth. Another mother in Georgia, Marsha Manatt, had already discovered just how many of the parties around her home, organised by teenagers, were drugs parties. The director of NIDA had also changed his mind about marijuana; parental concern, he later explained, not science, was the reason.

By 1978 even teenagers in America were shifting their ground. The belief that smoking marijuana was harmless was agreed by 65 per cent in 1978; by 1985 only 30 per cent agreed. General use of the drug began to drop off, too. This was among middle-class students, not the less advantaged. But the significance of this, as always, is that it would be middle-class values which would push for particular kinds of policy. The Carter years, and any hope that there might be a change of drugs policy direction, mark a time when things might have turned out very differently. They did not.

Also in 1978, the House of Representatives threw out the Senate Bill which would have revised the law on possession of marijuana. But even while this Bill was before the House, budgets for the drugs agencies were still rising. In 1977 they had reached $382 million (under President Ford); by 1981, the end of the Carter administration, they had reached $855 million. Under the next three presidents they would continue to rise, but now the rise would be meteoric, helped after the 1980s by the ending of the Cold War and the release of huge quantities of military cash, ripe for diversion. To put this into figures: by 1993 the drugs law enforcement budget in the United States had reached $7.8 billion and by this date the DEA, based in the Justice Department, was just one of 15 agencies or programmes involved in drugs law enforcement. Seven agencies were involved at the Treasury. At the Department of Defense the military budget for drugs enforcement had reached a billion dollars by this time. The growth of military involvement had by then broken the United States' deep-rooted convention about military intervention in domestic matters, which went back as far as the Civil War of the nineteenth century.

The whole cocaine game was about to go through a series of changes anyway, because by the late 1970s supplies of the drug were soaring and the price was dropping. Into the supplier frame were to come some of the nastiest people imaginable. From being a fun drug to use and have around, cocaine was to become increasingly identified with violent death, first in the supply chain and then, much more chillingly, in the way it was used.

10

CRACK'S IN THE DOOR

THE SUPPLY OF COCAINE IN THE 1960S had all but dried up. By the early 1970s, it was becoming more available but was still very expensive. Soon, though, the price would begin to fall. Even though the 'cuts' available to the buyers in the middle-class houses where it might well be delivered and the streets where it could fairly easily be found were variable, the quality would by and large remain high. The reasons why cocaine became so readily obtainable are simple: the crops of coca in South America are generally reliable and plentiful. The supply route to the north is relatively short, and the profits to be made from cocaine are such that smugglers are easy to find. There was already in place a short line route which was easy to extend across America. Finally, both South Americans and North Americans had no problems in co-operating in the first stages, to supply a drug which the consensus had decided was not going to create a moral – and thus major political or police – dilemma.

The short supply line had started because exiled Cubans, living in Miami after Castro came to power in 1959, had continued to smuggle and use cocaine after they fled the communist regime during the 1960s. Many were well off enough to afford the still highly priced drug; others were well versed in clandestine operations, because the CIA was constantly on the lookout for willing volunteers to infiltrate communist Cuba and had pumped in a lot of money for training and equipment. Guns, fast boats, all kinds of anti-surveillance gear and a local attitude which turned a blind eye to any other uses that this gear might be put to was of considerable help. Cuba was perceived in America as beyond the pale, and smuggling goods out of it of no real consequence. In the 1960s these smuggling activities – even of drugs – were small beer. No seizures of cocaine during this time exceeded 100 kilogrammes.

The traditional suppliers of cocaine at this time were Chilean, not Colombian, buying coca paste in the Andes, refining it in their small and crude laboratories and then sending it north to the Cubans, often in their traditional wicker wine baskets. As the business slowly expanded they occasionally used Colombian couriers, among others. While this small-time trade was taking place, a bigger smuggling operation was bringing in all kinds of goods from the north to South American countries with their very high taxes for imported goods. Among the electrical and electronic goods, cigarettes and alcohol were quantities of heroin, destined for return back to North America. This smuggling operation was controlled by Corsicans, part of the so-called French connection, memorably filmed with Gene Hackman in the starring role.

When this heroin connection was eventually broken up, the gap in drugs was taken up by marijuana at first and then, as it became more and more popular, cocaine. Now there was an expanding market for cocaine in the north and a ready supply chain in place. The Colombians, far closer to the North American coast and with a littoral on the Caribbean, were well placed to get directly involved in this hugely expanding market. First of all, they were able to supply better-quality, higher-strength marijuana. They were immeasurably helped in this by the Mexican government campaign to eradicate their own marijuana fields by spraying them with paraquat. The effect of this was to be devastating, but not in ways the devisers of this scheme in Mexico City and Washington intended. The main effect of the paraquat policy was to move the marijuana supply south, further away from the United States border but also further from any chance of drugs enforcement agencies in America easily monitoring what was going on. We may surmise that the policy may have pushed some marijuana users, worried about what they were smoking, towards snorting cocaine, produced as it was well beyond the crop-spraying aeroplanes in Mexico. Current efforts to spray fields of coca plants in South America remain as controversial as this earlier policy. It is easy to see why.

Ordinary Chileans might have stayed in their lucrative and growing business but for another American-inspired – although entirely unrelated to drugs – initiative. In the early 1970s the Chileans had elected the world's first avowed Marxist president, Salvador Allende. Almost immediately the United States began a sustained campaign to oust him by any means short of outright invasion. In 1973, finally, they were successful when Allende's government was overthrown in a short but bloody coup. What followed under the watchful and baleful eye of General Pinochet was far worse and, indeed, in 2001, is still a matter of international concern. Tens of thousands were tortured and many barbarically murdered.

For the Chilean drug smugglers the game was largely up, as drugs became another of the targets of the Chilean military regime. A target, but not in the way a casual observer might have thought. The trade in cocaine, as so often, proved too lucrative to suppress. Recent evidence has come to light to suggest that parts of the military regime in Chile moved in on the smugglers' patch and took at least some of their business over. Even General Pinochet has been implicated in this; unexplained large sums of money (up to three-quarters of a millon pounds) in an American bank account, in his and his wife's names, have come to light.

The Colombians, meanwhile, ever mindful of a business opportunity, also moved in, aided by a number of ex-military and well-trained American Vietnam veterans, often jobless and footloose, looking for ready cash and a bit of an adventure. Many were more than happy to turn their attention and skills to a highly profitable trade. Small, and not so small, aircraft joined the high-speed boats running up the coast of Miami to make their ever-increasing drops. Many of the Americans, like the Cuban exiles before, were putting to use the now-redundant skills they had been taught, in their case for Vietnam, which war finally ended in 1975 right in the middle of the new cocaine boom.

One of the early key Colombian players in the supply of cocaine was Carlos Rivas Lehder, who idolised a curious combination of Adolf Hitler, Che Guevara and John Lennon. He had met an American, George Jung, while both of them were in prison for smuggling marijuana. Jung had been caught while using an aircraft. Lehder realised the method could be used to smuggle in huge quantities of cocaine, yielding unreal profits. Among other ideas, Lehder wanted to get into Colombian politics – maybe even run for president – and that took lots of cash.

When they left prison Jung and Lehder went into the cocaine business together. Within a short time they had half a dozen pilots flying quarter-tonne loads of cocaine into landing strips in Florida, Georgia and the Carolinas. Their 'staff' were all ex-navy or airforce veterans. Back in Colombia a small town – Medellin – became the preferred base for many of the cocaine traffickers, who felt safer in numbers; their number was now rapidly growing.

Their number was growing, too, in the United States, particularly in the

Jackson Heights, Queens, area of New York. The Colombians there quickly became known for their savage way of dealing with anyone or anything that got in their way. In one case, a group raided the home of a well-known Colombian cocaine dealer, Oscar Toro. They stole all his money, kidnapped his ten-year-old son and the babysitter and hanged Toro's five-year-old daughter on the spot. When the son was found by the police he was dead – strangled. The babysitter found with him had been repeatedly raped and then strangled too. Toro refused point blank to help the police.

Colombia had long had a reputation for violence and for degrees of corruption shocking even in a continent known for its bribery. Distribution of wealth between rich and poor was much worse than in neighbouring countries. A cash crop like coca – not that by any means the majority is grown there – was good news. Even so, for the peasants who grew it the advantage was small. But for those smart and ruthless enough, the illegal cocaine trade would create wealth on a scale hardly to be credited. With it would come the potential for huge bribes running through the country from top to bottom. The entire system of government in Colombia has been implicated from time to time: politicians, police, military and the justice system. When bribes could not be made to work, kidnap, torture of increasingly grim kinds, or straightforward murder worked instead.

The country, long wracked by a series of civil wars, has been torn asunder time and again. Nothing on this scale had been seen before in South America. The violence spilled out in all directions; it came, of course, to the United States, notably first to Florida. In 1979 there was more than one drugs killing a day in Miami, where there were 379 murders that year; by 1981 this had increased to 621, a quarter committed by automatic weapons. Between 1975 and 1980, 220,000 guns were sold in Dade County alone. In 1981 alone, 66,000 guns were sold. At the same time the state's banking system was going completely crazy with banks receiving – in suitcase-loads at a time – extraordinary quantities of unexplained cash. In one small area of Miami banks showed a combined surplus in one year of $3.3 billion; by 1980 that was up to well over $6 billion. In the same year the Drugs Enforcement Agency estimated the drugs business in Florida was yielding $7 billion a year, clearly outrunning the tourist trade (at $5 billion).

Back in Colombia, major players in this by now worldwide business were still able to act with relative impunity. Pablo Escobar, perhaps the most notorious of all traffickers, easily obtained a visa from the US embassy in Bogota to visit America. Later he would become a deputy in the Colombian parliament. Escobar was finally murdered in 1993, but there have always been plenty of others ready and willing to step into the place held by any of the major suppliers – the money is just too good. The major players in Colombia keep themselves on the right side of many of the people by providing hospitals, schools and other public works, and helping out with an infrastructure which successive governments had signally failed to provide. They also created work in the coca plantations and the many laboratories processing the leaves, in the vast private security forces they needed, and in the whole transport system they put together to get the cocaine out of the country. By 1983, 20 tonnes of cocaine a month was being produced by a single large compound built on a river island deep in Colombia's rain forest. But, like medieval barons, they enforced all this with a level of actual and implicit violence that prevented the vast majority of ordinary people from doing very much to stop them. The 'official' government remained besieged in Bogota, assisted by American arms and, increasingly, by on the ground 'advisers'.

Still as popular as ever in the United States and increasingly in the rest of the world, cocaine in the 1970s was mostly taken in the usual way – straight up the nose by way of a rolled banknote, preferably of a large denomination. There had always been other ways of taking cocaine: injecting it was one of the other early methods. No one seems to know quite when snorting became popular. Smoking ordinary cocaine is not possible: it decomposes at the temperature required to vaporise it, but sometime in the 1970s a new form of cocaine was devised: freebase, which could be smoked.

This form provided a massive rush for the user; far, far stronger than with the snorted powder, which has a natural falling off as the blood vessels in the mucous membranes in the nose constrict (see the Appendix). Many of those who have tried smoking freebase cocaine, even just a few times, say it is the most exquisite feeling they have ever had. The current view of smoking cocaine, either as freebase or as crack, is that it is certainly a lot more effective at providing a very fast hit, but that by and large early fears of its terrible addictive qualities were, like so much to do with drugs, wildly exaggerated. While powdered cocaine will deliver a hit inside about 20 minutes, freebase (and crack) do the same within minutes. Some have spoken of a 'whole body orgasm'.

The first freebase kit for the extraction of freebase cocaine from cocaine hydrochloride was developed by Paraphernalia HQ of California, where this new trend appears to have begun in 1978. By early 1979, advertisements for pipes and kits were appearing in underground magazines and newspapers. Freebase cocaine can be made using volatile solvents, but this is highly dangerous as they may well ignite during the process; Richard Prior, the US comedian, was found on fire rushing from his house after trying to prepare freebase with highly inflammable ether. Freebase in its first manifestation was much in vogue in Hollywood and the surrounding parts of California in the late 1970s. It was expensive and difficult to make using this process.

More convenient, and much safer, methods of making freebase cocaine involve either ammonia or baking powder. To obtain crack cocaine using the latter, ordinary cocaine hydrochloride is concentrated by heating it in a solution of baking soda until the water evaporates. The base-cocaine thus obtained makes a cracking sound when it is heated. It vaporises at a much lower temperature than the hydrochloride and it can easily be inhaled using a pipe. Using ammonia will result in a purer form, as will using ether, but both are longer and more difficult processes, which is why crack became so much more readily available in the 1980s in America.

Prices for cocaine were dropping at this time as more and more came on the market and, apart from users realising they could get a better hit from smoking it, suppliers also came to realise that those who did usually wanted much more at one time than if they were using the powder. As well, in a highly adulterated form (such as crack) it could be sold cheaply, thereby expanding the market downwards. All in all, cocaine was now entering a new phase, which might be likened to the 'upgrade' between opium and morphine, or morphine and heroin, although in every other respect the result was a severe downgrade. On price the situation was close to insanity. If powder could be bought for $75 a gramme (about £50), a small crack 'rock' would cost $5 (£3). The difference, a key one, was that you kept on wanting crack . . . and wanting it . . . and wanting it. Smoking up to 50 rocks at a session was not uncommon. At that level the prices reverse; most powder users might get through two grammes (at about £100); 50 rocks could cost 50 per cent more. As users tend to be poor, the only way they can sustain that level of use is to get the money by stealing. Cocaine, in this form, took on the same mantle as heroin: a drug which created crime in its own right.

Smoking cocaine has taken two routes: the middle-class smoke freebase; the poor smoke crack (although there are overlaps). The key to what happened with regards to cocaine in the late 1980s in America, and to a far lesser extent in Britain from the 1990s onwards, once more takes us back to some of the darker aspects surrounding cocaine and race. To put it a different way, one which to some degree may be found in popular press accounts: if cocaine powder is a bit naughty and sometimes might even be a laugh, crack cocaine has to be suppressed at all costs because poor blacks are using it to get high, then going out to steal and cause mayhem. In the United States there was a huge increase in violence surrounding the crack epidemic, caused in many cases by rivalry between drug-dealing gangs and their territories. The result for many inner-city areas in America was urban warfare on a scale not seen before.

The wars on the streets coincided with the middle period of the Reagan years. By the time he came to the White House in 1981, it was cocaine which had become the priority for drugs control agencies; NIDA had estimated that cocaine use tripled between 1977 and 1979 and that by 1980 the number of cocaine powder sellers in New York outnumbered heroin sellers by two to one. Reagan's two-term administration was elected through a populist right-wing base and almost everything he was able to do to demonstrate a harder and harder line on drugs use was applauded. Nancy Reagan also stepped into the public domain by taking up a personal campaign against drug use: 'Just say no' was her message. She also said: 'Each of us has a responsibility to be intolerant of drug use anywhere, any time, by anybody. We must create an atmosphere of intolerance for drug use in this country.'

Money for research into drugs or treatment programmes dropped dramatically as money for law enforcement rose. Nothing, though, appeared to stem the quantity of drugs available on the street. This was also a time when the wholesale price of cocaine was tumbling from $60,000 a kilogramme in the late 1970s to around $15–20,000 by the mid-1980s. The quality of the cocaine was getting better, too, notwithstanding the onset of crack cocaine.

The fall in price was the result of the huge increase in use by middle-class America in the 1970s, coupled with the ever-increasing efforts by suppliers in South America. Use of cocaine appears to have peaked in 1980, when nearly 20 per cent of those aged 15–25 admitted using it. But this presaged a steep decline and it was on the back of this decline that the crack explosion began. Cocaine manufacturers, now with a glut on their hands, sought ways to reduce its price and increase its use. Crack was the answer: cheap freebase coming to a ghetto near you! Against this pressure, the Reagan administrations could do little except go on raising the financial drugs enforcement stakes. In 1986, the government announced it was, as had happened so many times before, looking at reducing demand. Even so, most of the 1986 $4 billion resulting from the Anti-Drug Abuse Act of that year went into an intensified law enforcement campaign at home.

There were other changes, ones which we have now begun to inherit all over Europe. Taking an entirely different tack, drugs testing of employees began in a number of commercial organisations. First used by the military to test returning personnel from Vietnam, mostly for heroin, new tests were being developed which were much more sensitive and could discover if the person being tested had used any number of substances. The problem that would emerge from these tests was that drugs like marijuana remain in the bloodstream for very much longer than, for instance, cocaine – or heroin. The temptation to use these drugs, rather than get caught out using marijuana, would prove irresistible, especially in closed institutions like prisons. Once more, the efforts to control drugs through draconian and prohibitive regulations would backfire.

Whilst the domestic battle was raging, other approaches were being made, ones which have become far more sinister because, once again, they have created a new kind of cold warrior attitude to the rest of the world. By the end of 1981 Reagan had issued an executive order demanding that the entire federal intelligence apparatus, within which falls the CIA, must provide assistance in the new drugs war now officially declared. For the first time since the Civil War Reagan also got the military directly involved in domestic policy enforcement, arguing in an amendment to the existing law that the Navy ought to join civilian agencies, like the Coastguard, in stopping vessels at sea suspected of drugs smuggling. All other branches of the armed services were empowered to assist the Customs, Coastguard and the DEA. The money for the military's part in all this would rise from $5 million in 1982 to over one billion dollars in the 1990s.

In January 1982 Reagan created the South Florida Task Force, led by Vice-President George Bush, to coordinate drugs busting in the region through which the vast bulk of the cocaine was coming. In the same year Reagan had addressed the heads of 18 agencies, along with military leaders and the IRS Commissioner, to say:

> We are rejecting the helpless attitude that drug use is so rampant that
> we are defenseless to do anything about it. We are taking down the
> surrender flag that has flown over so many drug efforts; we are running
> up the battle flag. We can fight the drug problem and we can win.

Twelve more Florida-style task forces had been set up by 1984, now involving
agencies as diverse as the DEA, Customs, the FBI, Internal Revenue, the US
Marshals Service and the Bureau of Alcohol, Tobacco and Firearms (ATF).
The high-profile Reagan campaign was helped by the media, now alerted to
the crack problem in the big cities. A moral panic ensued, lasting until the end
of the 1980s, with many resonances of the previous panic over cocaine of the
1900s. Once more it was suggested that crack users had superhuman powers
to resist arrest, even being able to resist bullets if shot by the police. A law of
1986 even went so far as to overtly discriminate against the largely black crack
users. The Anti-Drug Act specified that there should be a minimum sentence
of ten years for being in possession of 50 grammes of crack; for powdered
cocaine you would have to be caught with 10 *kilogrammes*, 100 times as much.
The official reasoning was that crack was far more addictive – but powdered
cocaine can, of course, be dissolved and injected, making it just as addictive,
along with the added danger of HIV/Aids infection.

By 1985 use of crack cocaine had spread to many of the major cities in the
United States. Crack smokers were completely different from cocaine users. The
majority were to be found in the most deprived black and Hispanic neighbour-
hoods. For the street dealers, like the black youngsters who had few if any job
prospects, selling crack was no choice at all: you did it if you could get hold of it.
This business had huge advantages: large quantities of cash in hand, no white
bosses, no taxes to pay, no arguments about dress or attitude, no qualifications
(except possibly the ability to fire a gun). By the late 1980s armed crack gangs
were common; happy, like their Colombian (and now Caribbean) suppliers to
launch murderous automatic gunfire attacks on anyone who got in their way.

Crack attracted an unusually high number of women users; the image was
not, this time, though, an effete one of a gentile middle- or lower middle-class
woman with a nervous demeanour. One American drugs researcher, James
Inciardi, found this scene when he visited a 'crack house' in Miami:

> I observed what apppeared to be the forcible gang-rape of an
> unconscious child. Emaciated, seemingly comatose, and likely to be no

more than fourteen years of age, she was lying spreadeagled on a filthy mattress while four men in succession had vaginal intercourse with her. Despite what was happening, I was urged not to interfere. After they had finished and left the room, another man came in, and they engaged in oral sex.

He was told she was a house girl, which meant the house owner gave her food, drink, a place to sleep and all the crack she wanted in return for giving as much sex as was required by the customers he had. Inciardi said he felt the pure depravity of it was 'deeply disturbing'.

This kind of activity gave rise to what were known as 'crack babies', born on the back of the 'freak' houses, like the one described here, where a woman would perform any form of intercourse, oral, anal, unprotected vaginal, for access to crack. Having seen to some extent that people took up smoking freebase because it created a high with cocaine only otherwise to be attained through injection with its HIV risk, by the late 1980s the crack epidemic was making its own sad contribution to the HIV/Aids infections through the older route of unprotected sex.

Crack use in the United States peaked in late 1980s. Its use appears to have died down less because of the huge efforts made by enforcement agencies, and more because, like most drugs fashions, use eventually declines to a hard core of abusers or addicts. As with most things American, crack came to Britain and we will look at that in the final chapter.

When George Bush entered the White House in 1989, he merely intensified the previous Reagan approach. A former director of the CIA, he had no problem with their involvement in any of his drugs policies, even though by now the murky instances of intelligence agency support for the Contras, who were in many cases dealing in cocaine, were beginning to emerge. This was not a new departure. Long before Vietnam, in the early 1950s, the CIA had helped anti-communist groups known to be dealing in heroin, just as they had helped others later in south-east Asia. The communist threat was always deemed to be the greater and it had meant differing parts of the United States government machine were in effect fighting themselves.

Bush's first televised address to America in the autumn of 1989 announced: 'All of us agree that the gravest domestic threat facing our nation today is drugs . . . victory over drugs is our cause, a just cause . . . Who is responsible?

Let me tell you straight out. Everyone who uses drugs. Everyone who sells drugs. And everyone who looks the other way.' He went on: 'The rules have changed: if you sell drugs you will be caught; and when you are caught, you will be prosecuted; and once you are convicted, you will do time. Caught, prosecuted, punished.' He specifically added: 'American cocaine users need to understand that our nation has zero tolerance for casual drug use.' Finally, Bush said that his government would make the entire US military machine available in this battle, at home and abroad.

There was an awful logic in all of this, which would lead within a couple of years to the huge resources of America's military power, hitherto deployed against the now more-or-less non-existent threat from communism or those nation states who had embraced it, shifting their ground to fighting drug supplies. The fight would move away from the American coastline to South America, notably Colombia. It would involve direct military intervention to capture the Panamian General Noriega, a former 'friend' of the United States, and would result in his imprisonment in Florida.

The logic of this approach meant that elected officials would declare that anything went if drugs trafficking could be stopped. The President appointed a drugs 'csar' who happily told a national radio audience that there was nothing morally wrong with beheading drug traffickers. The Bush administration itself returned to the proposition that the death penalty should be used against large-scale traffickers and a former United States customs chief said that aeroplanes even just suspected of carrying drugs should be shot down. Forty-eight members of the United States Senate agreed with him. All this had a huge impact on American public opinion. In July 1989, only 20 per cent of those asked in an opinion poll said that drugs were the most important problem facing America. Two months later, after Bush's major speech (quoted above), that figure had risen to 64 per cent. Bush, meanwhile, had been seen on television holding up a bag of crack. The message was was clear enough: if I can get it from around the White House, as sure as heck it is in your neighbourhood, too.

If the Reagan and Bush years witnessed a huge expansion in drugs enforcement and the policies which go along with it, the last eight years of the twentieth century, under Clinton administrations, have not seen any form of rollback; either in terms of budget or in the numbers of those engaged in this unwinnable war. Early on Clinton's own drugs csar, Lee Brown, had said: 'You won't hear us using the metaphor "drugs war". We should help those who need help and arrest those who are trafficking in drugs. But I don't think we should declare war against our own people.'

Whilst he could happily say this, the figures showed that whereas in 1990 there had been 1,089,500 Americans arrested for drugs violations, in 1993 1,126,300 Americans were arrested. Seizures of drugs continued to rise as well but the most startling figures come from continuing budgetary increases, as well as the numbers of government departments and agencies fighting the now officially declared non-existent war.

By the mid-1990s the DEA was still the lead agency, but its $800 million budget was just 10 per cent of the total committed. The DEA now had well over 6,000 employees, including over 3,000 special agents in more than 170 offices in the United States and in 48 countries abroad. Its reach could be long. Howard Marks, a major British drugs dealer in marijuana, fell foul of the DEA although he never dealt directly in America. Despite this, the DEA managed to get him extradited from Spain to America, where he served time.

A huge part of the United States' government machine is devoted to drugs enforcement policies. Here is a glimpse into how it works: the FBI conduct investigations into trafficking. The Immigration Service try to stop drug smugglers at the border; the US Marshals Service get money for judicial security, transporting prisoners, apprehending suspects and managing seized assets. The United States Customs Service are charged with stopping the flow of drugs by air, sea and land; the Internal Revenue Service has a role in identifying and stopping the transfer of drug-related funds, and investigating and disrupt money-laundering. The Pentagon provides support to the law enforcement agencies that have counter-drug responsibilities; half of the North American Aerospace Defense Command, created to track Soviet missiles and aircraft, is devoted to targeting drugs smugglers. The United States Southern Command has been reorganised to fight the drugs war in Latin America and the military are increasingly locked into a Vietnam-style role in Colombia. National guardsmen across the United States search cargoes, patrol borders, fly surveillance missions and destroy locally grown marijuana crops.

More prosaically, the Department of Agriculture Forest Service investigate marijuana production and fund research into herbicides that will be specific to drugs crops – of which the coca plant is top of the current list. All of this complex activity, with its annual requests for money (always, but always, more) has created a sprawling narco-enforcement complex, the like of which those framers of the Harrison Act could never have imagined.

There is little sign that any of it is stopping, let alone addressing, the issues which are central to drug-taking, or to the chronic problem of drug abuse. There is equally little sign that a worldwide industry which is estimated to take up to 8 per cent of world GDP, along with legal industries like oil, gas and tourism, is much affected by all the sound and fury this generates. But the American drug enforcement juggernaut, like the mighty Mississippi, just keeps rolling along, dragging in its wake an increasing number of victims, both in terms of the treatment they do not get to stop their habits, or the treatment they do get from a prison system overladen with drugs offenders, overwhelmingly of the lesser kind.

The last words in this chapter should go to the latest reports from the front-line – Colombia – where there is absolutely no sign that American involvement is anything other than on the increase. Colombia still turns out more than 70 per cent of the world's cocaine, although there is a strong likelihood that new production may once again be beginning to start up in Indonesia (old Dutch Java), where the yields were always high and the geography (thousands of small, densely foliated islands) makes detection much harder. In Colombia, United States aid has grown ten-fold since 1995: in 1999 it received $366 million in equipment and training for drugs enforcement. The largest part of this will go toward the loan and maintenance of 63 helicopters.

If we are to make a comparison with America's last big long-term war – Vietnam – which they lost after a huge investment in lives and materials, there is one vital difference. In Vietnam, the Americans lost because they failed to understand they were not fighting a communist conspiracy but a national movement for independence and integration. In the end it mattered little to the Americans; their method of approach was entirely misplaced.

In Colombia the Americans are fighting something much more diffuse, a product the rest of the world shows little sign – unlike the creed of communism – of rejecting. The Colombian economy is distorted by cocaine, but it is based on a capitalist system which worships free enterprise, including the freedom of people everywhere to make choices about which products they wish to consume. The Americans are, in one sense, fighting their own creed this time round, not some alien one. Cocaine is a product largely going to the United States, where people in large numbers have made it all too clear what their choice will be, even if they could be persuaded to eliminate crack cocaine from their lives. Cocaine is not being forced onto reluctant consumers who then get 'hooked'.

It is just conceivable that America might win its drugs war in Colombia, but the underlying problem will remain because production can always be moved. America and American drugs enforcement policies, like those stratagems of the Pentagon in the 1970s, are most likely doomed once more. The question is, when will this become apparent to the policy-makers?

11

COCAINE'S ENDLESS ENCORE

THE UN DECADE AGAINST DRUG ABUSE: 1991–2000

PERHAPS THE OFFICIALS WHO DEVISED the term 'Decade against Drug Abuse' consciously recognised what it would spell; perhaps not. But DADA is a potent metaphoric acronym for the chaotic, often contradictory, situation in worldwide illegal drugs enforcement policy, just as the artistic movement which bore the same name symbolised anarchy and nonsense. It is time to start to look at the big picture; not the one foisted upon us by a largely American agenda, but one which takes into account all that we know about recreational drug use and abuse, and which sees this as an expanding market that is not going to close.

The main beneficiaries from the current situation are the suppliers: criminals. Well, up to a point. For we have also seen the rise of a huge legal 'industry' of police and military agencies, research institutions and treatment centres, disparate in aims, often in conflict, all vying for funds as well as public attention. And then there are the recreational drug users in their millions: people who have been firmly placed on the criminal side of the law, for this is not something akin to speeding or fiddling a few expenses at work. Finally, but never to be forgotten, are the real victims in the present mess, drug users who cannot control their habit and for whom each day dawns as a miserable reminder that they have to find more supplies of whatever drug they cannot do without.

This latter group is only a small proportion of a huge number of addicts who cannot rid themselves of that most insidious of drugs, alcohol. Unlike alcoholics, other drug abusers are vilified by and large as criminal losers; many, indeed, will commit crimes to feed their habit. Others, largely but by no means exclusively women, will come to allow their bodies to be exploited and abused by others in order to get the drugs they crave. They may well pass on their problems to their children through HIV/Aids, or through physical or psychological damage through drug use in pregnancy.

Running as a thick seam through all this, and applicable in particular to cocaine, is media coverage. This veers between a 'shock! horror!' attitude towards the drugs issue at a very basic street level (and therefore, often the poverty end of the scale with all its attendant social ills) and 'semi-shock', often tinged with what might be called a 'tut tut' attitude, towards use of drugs by the rich and famous. Cocaine occupies a unique role here, because its expense has meant that affluent users create a curiously envious sub-text: those who can afford to use it whenever they feel like it are seen to be winners in all other aspects of life's game.

We are home now, back in Britain. The United States may have started the first great cocaine fever; it may dictate much of the world's enforcement policies, but back here, we have not yet reached the violently reactive stage against cocaine that took place in the 1980s after crack made its first appearance. One reason is that a similar epidemic, predicted by some in the early 1990s, is unlikely to develop here.

Many now accept that the American experience with crack cocaine was less to do with its extreme addictiveness, more to do with high baseline rates of drug use, including cocaine; proximity to the producers in South America; and a much higher level of street violence in the United States prior to its arrival. British users of the powder (cocaine hydrochloride) were associated strongly with winners in the 1980s, not losers. Despite some high-profile abusers and their tales of woe as expressed in the tabloids, cocaine has failed to get the very bad press here that it has in the United States. Partly, this may be explained by reference to its relatively small constituency of use in Britain; partly, perhaps, to a cultural 'groundedness' which somehow manages to take up a fad – frequently American in origin – but not go utterly ape for it.

Despite our common language and, to some extent in the past, culture, Britain is a very different society to America – much closer, as we have latterly begun to realise, to Europe. It may well be because of our tolerance to what is sometimes seen as eccentric rather than criminal behaviour that it is possible for writers like Will Self to admit to having used heroin and yet still be entirely acceptable within the confines of their present lives. There is here a powerful resonance which runs back to de Quincey or Coleridge, a benign rather than a moralistic or punitive one, as is often the case in America. As far as cocaine goes, it could be argued that this has to do with who gets to take it. It is still overwhelmingly a middle-class, professional, city-slicker indulgence or, and this is crucial, an indulgence of people in the entertainment industries and the mass media. This latter attitude means that the likes of Julie Burchill, at the drop of a column in the *Guardian*, will feel free to boast of her use of cocaine. Many others have done likewise.

The paper-thin veneer used in discussing this (or any other drug) is 'I used to take it', in which case the quantities are likely to be bumped up (much as in William Hague's '14-pints-of-beer-drunk-at-one-session' boast). With long-past use, sometimes admitted to with a requisite amount of contrition, goes a kind of socially acceptable sigh over the ways of callow youth.

By 1999, from official figures supplied by the National Criminal Intelligence Service, cocaine users had outstripped heroin users for the first time. The NCIS did not supply figures to back its claim, but researchers at Liverpool University suggest that there are probably around 600,000 regular cocaine users, compared with 250,000 heroin users.

Cocaine has retained its image as the champagne drug here despite the arrival of crack. If anything, cocaine as powder is regarded as an expensive, naughty but nice, adjunct to many a good evening out. Some of the more chic dinner parties across Britain will bring a little 'charlie' out at the end of a meal. I used to believe this was mythological, rather in the way of your average urban myth; it is not. Cocaine is fairly easy to get hold of in today's Britain and, no doubt, Europe. The quality is usually good and the price has remained steady for years. As I described at the beginnning of this book, intriguingly, in remarking in many contexts and places that I was writing it, many people who claim not to have tried cocaine have expressed a desire to 'have a go'.

The upsurge in cocaine use has meant a change in the way it is supplied, the new-style dealers profiting from a 750 per cent increase of use over the past ten years. These new dealers will trade in quantities of up to £100,000 a time, using every facility available, such as the internet as well as state-of-the-art anti-surveillance techniques, to stay ahead of the authorities. One estimate has one dealer for every three users, a total of 20,000 dealers. They will be supplied by a few dozen 'wholesale' distributors, themselves supplied by two or three large-scale operators. Many – if not most – of those involved in supplying cocaine in the UK will not take it; many will not even drink alcohol, treating this as strictly business.

As for supply, traditionally shipments came in directly from Colombia via Panama, Argentina, Brazil, Venezuela and the Caribbean. More recently new routes have opened up via South Africa and countries in west Africa. In the past couple of years the Balkans, and eastern Europe in general, have been identified as routes of passage for cocaine arriving in western Europe. Small consignments come through the Channel Tunnel (20 kilogrammes or less); larger shipments come in containers, by air or by sea, or are hidden in the larger lorries crossing by ferry or by Channel Tunnel trains.

As the development of cocaine use in Britain, and much of Europe, has been and continues to be very different from that which has happened in the United States, we need to take a final closer look at the British experience of it since the 1920s and how the authorities here have dealt with it. Four times in the past hundred years it has figured as an issue of concern: the first was the scare of 1916, when the Defence of the Realm Act was amended.

The second time was during the 1920s when, as noted before, the 'smart set' used it, again with little evidence off widespread abuse. This was at a time when, post-war, all things American were being snapped up, especially anything related to entertainment; ironic, then, that the United States' own problem with cocaine had already more or less ended. But put into context, cocaine use in Britain was very limited in the 1920s. Even so, there was then a racial dimension in public reactions to its use.

A third cocaine scare came during the 1960s when a small number of heroin users were getting cocaine on prescription. To put this into perspective, between 1959 and 1964 it is believed that the number of cocaine 'addicts' in Britain had increased from 30 to 211 (a seven-fold increase, if the alarmist view is taken, but hardly an issue if actual numbers are considered). There is a question mark, too, over the term 'addict', when applied to these numbers. Data are rare; so then was cocaine.

It is to the final period, the one in which we live, that most attention has to be turned. If there ever has been a cocaine fever in Britain, or anything approaching it, now is the time – the period running from the 1980s, the Thatcher years, with which its high-rolling image will be forever associated. At the start of the 1990s a scare began, carefully fostered by parts of the government, police and other agencies, over the imminent onset of a crack epidemic. Whilst there is no doubt that crack use is on the increase and that it does lead to extremes of violence, in which gangs such as the Jamaican-based Yardies are involved, it has not led to the kinds of predicted out-and-out warfare seen in parts of the United States 15 years ago. Nor, despite recent fears about the extent to which guns are now part of British drug culture, is there likely to be, for reasons outlined earlier.

The British attitude to drugs control has often followed that of the United States; but not on every occasion. After the amendment to the Defence of the Realm Act in 1916, the 1920 Dangerous Drugs Act brought in a unified system to deal with cocaine, heroin, morphine and opium. It was cocaine use, associated with the 'living for kicks' frenetic society of the 1920s and the fact that it was the most popular street drug of the time, that led to the Dangerous Drugs (Amendment) Act of 1923. This increased the penalties for possession and supply and gave the police wide powers of search. Following concerns about prescribing policies by doctors to heroin users, the same users who were also getting cocaine, the Dangerous Drugs Act 1967 was passed which, among other things, limited the prescribing of cocaine to addicts by doctors; by 1969 this line of supply had more or less completely dried up.

The 1970s and, more significantly, 1980s cocaine scare in the United States led to a House of Commons Home Affairs Committee inquiring into the use of 'hard' drugs. They went to America where they discovered 'the most devastating drug there today is cocaine . . . turning respectable people into criminals to satisfy a craving which dominates all other appetites' (one may make a reasonable assumption here that they were talking about crack). The Committee was worried that as the United States market became saturated, so Britain and Europe would be targeted by suppliers. The subsequent Drug Trafficking Offences Act of 1986 allowed for the freezing of assets of convicted drug traffickers and the confiscation of any profits made this way. But Britain in the 1980s had a much bigger cheaply available heroin problem than it ever did a cocaine one.

Research has suggested that as late as 1985, cocaine was not a 'street' drug at all but that it retained its luxury image by being used by a 'substantial upmarket clientele within advertising, journalism, popular entertainment, business and socialite circles'. Working-class drug users were still mostly wedded to amphetamines which were a lot cheaper (and nastier). But the latter part of the 1980s saw the growth of the huge rave party movement and a massive increase in use of another drug altogether: MDMA or, as it was later to be dubbed, ecstasy. First developed in Germany in 1912 by, of all companies, Merck, probably as a slimming pill, it was much later tested by the American military, along with LSD and the rest, to see if it could be used to disorientate the enemy. Later still some psychotherapists, also in the United States, thought it might help couples learn to relate better to one another. By the early 1980s its effects were becoming widely known. Brought to Europe, it was almost overnight transformed into the hugely popular dance drug it has remained. British youth were largely responsible for this; the Americans have never used it in anything like the same quantities. Ecstasy's arriving when it did may well have stopped a cocaine craze developing among young people in Europe, as it had in America.

Ecstasy has remained one of the more controversial of the wholly manufactured drugs (that is, unlike cocaine, it has no known natural derivative). Associated chemically with the amphetamine group, it has also been the centre of a controversy over whether it can in any way be lethal to a user, or whether unspecified prolonged use will later lead to chronic depression. Far more in daily and weekly use, and a lot cheaper than cocaine hydrochloride, its fascination for the dance-crazed Europeans probably continues to make a lasting impact on the way in which cocaine and crack cocaine are absorbed into British and European drug-taking cultures.

But while use of ecstasy was a major issue in the late 1980s and early 1990s, cocaine use was creeping up; prices have remained stable and, as already mentioned, its image – excluding crack cocaine – has hardly ever changed. By the late 1990s there was talk of an epidemic of use of the hydrochloride. In 1997, for example, there had been an increase of 25 per cent of arrests for cocaine possession on the year before: up to 4,500 from 3,400. Purity levels of seized cocaine were up too, to an average of 63 per cent from 51 per cent. Seizures had increased from 2,300 kilogrammes in 1996 to over 3,000 kilogrammes in 1997. With prices remaining at about £50 a gramme, many dealers were offering £20 'specials' for those who wanted a clubbing alternative to ecstasy. As with many experiences with recreational drugs, this latter offer was related to drug-user fears engendered by high-profile cases, such as that of Leah Betts. Fears over ecstasy made switching to cocaine an easy choice, even when the evidence that ecstasy was dangerous was as badly presented, or not proven, as it was in the Betts case.

Use of cocaine was by 1999 so widespread among many urban professionals as to hardly cause comment. Adam Edwards, son of a judge, former editor of a London magazine and an admitted cocaine user, wrote in the *Daily Mail* in May, 1999:

> The most surprising thing about Tom Parker Bowles [son of Camilla, the mistress of Prince Charles] admitting he took cocaine is that anyone is surprised. It would be more surprising if he had not taken the drug.
>
> Cocaine is the currency of the capital . . . In the past year, I have seen it taken by a Conservative politician, several lobbyists, a Guards officer, two QCs, a solicitor, a senior stockbroker, a merchant banker, and a score of media men and women, including PRs, publishers, writers, Fleet Street executives and television and film producers.

Sensationalist and breathy prose like this only provides a small insight into the reality. Edwards suggested that the key point was that there was no big deal in either taking cocaine openly at certain gatherings or passing it around, allied with the usual hypocrisy of '"I don't want my children to know I take drugs," said one of London's most notorious and beautiful aristocrats.' This harks back to the 1920s, as one might expect, but it does point to a trend: cocaine is now very much a recreational drug of choice for a growing number of people, by no means all city-dwellers or high fliers.

Serious research, rather than anecdote, points in the same direction. The British Crime Survey for 1999 revealed a 'significant' increase in all the indicators for cocaine use in the UK: 6 per cent of 16–29 year-olds said they had tried it. The figure for crack and heroin was just 1 per cent. It was suggested that up to 25 per cent of clubbers had tried it. Purity of cocaine powder has varied between 43 per cent and 59 per cent (for crack it has stayed much higher, at around 85 per cent) between 1992 and 1998. As a comparison, heroin purity varied between 29 per cent and 48 per cent; amphetamines tested were on average below 10 per cent (no surprise: amphetamines remain as the hidden problem drug); average MDMA (ecstasy) content per tablet was 80mg. Although the price of cocaine per gramme has remained stable in the UK, rising ever so slightly with inflation, its wholesale price per kilogramme is as much as 10–20 per cent higher than for the rest of Europe. As with so many consumer goods, it seems the British are as ill-dealt here as with cars or food in the European Union.

There are other drugs which might be added to the list – new drugs and variations of old ones (like skunk cannabis). There are, too, legal drugs with unimpeachable pedigrees for treating medical conditions: Prozac and Viagra come to mind, much as Valium and Temazepan do for a slightly earlier era. We live, truly, in a chemical world where our stresses and strains may, from time to time, only find relief in whatever drug we can obtain. There is no age limit in this search, or desire. Although youth is still overwhelmingly associated with drug use, especially over-use, it is only because of the twin and universal aspects of youthful desire to try anything once, with an often equal desire for inconsequential over-indulgence. Adult society worries itself sick over youth and its indulgences, whilst continuing to provide the means by which the young can (legally) get off their heads (using alcohol), adding an envious tinge to whatever excesses make the morning papers or breakfast television. At the same time adult society frets, as it must, over the image portrayed by youthful icons like sports stars or pop stars and their thoughtless, not to say downright stupid, commentaries on their own over-indulgent lives.

It is time we all grew up, painful though the process will be. But the pain will not be in witnessing the destruction of society by a massive and eventually fatal over-use by billions (rather than millions) of people, hell-bent on becoming addicted to cocaine, heroin, ecstasy or cannabis, or whatever newly synthesised drug is just around the corner. I make no distinction between these major recreational drugs, as the total abolitionists do, or the original American prohibitionists against alcohol did. Drugs are drugs are drugs. What we have to address is what we are going to do to change from the almost total quagmire of current thinking, policy and even use, to something akin to reality. A move which ought to take us a jot closer to science, as well as to common sense.

At the start of the twenty-first-century, Britain, like most of the rest of Europe, is following the same tired old route of prohibition and law enforcement. The notable exception, much written and talked about, is Holland, where a more relaxed attitude – although one widely misunderstood outside the Netherlands – operates with regard to marijuana and, to some extent, the unofficial quality control of ecstasy. The Dutch cannot detach themselves from the same international treaties which bind Britain and the rest, but they are at least trying to take a more pragmatic stance. What happens in Holland is closer to what the Americans might have done had they followed through the Bourne–Carter proposals of the 1970s. The Dutch provide a small beacon in an otherwise entirely unlit landscape.

In Britain, which according to recent surveys tops the European drugs league, there is little sign that anything will change for a long time. The Labour government which came to power in 1997 showed no sign of shifting the ground on drugs; if anything it acted to tighten the existing laws, with individual ministers falling over themselves to prove how tough they could be on drugs.

The British drugs 'csar' Keith Hallawell, while at times appearing to soften his approach, in general kept to the hard line that drug use was always wrong and that all drug-taking needed to be stamped out. Various senior police officers have, from time to time, suggested a softer approach, usually going on the record after they have retired. One or two have even said that the current policy was not working and ought to be abandoned. A few have said there is a case to be made for some drugs to be decriminalised (or at least that this should be looked at in some formal way). But when ministers such as Clare Short have put their heads over the parapet and tried to discuss, in the mildest terms, the question of decriminalising personal use of marijuana, for example, they have been comprehensively vilified.

No one in public life has seriously suggested that a fundamental re-thinking of the entire issue needs to be addressed, although late in 2000, in an attempt to raise the profile of the Conservative Party as a defender of freedom, William Hague appeared to call for a serious debate about drugs during the coming general election campaign. Elements of the libertarian right-wing of the Conservative Party would legalise all drugs on the grounds that their use is precisely a choice for individuals. Few – at this time – take this proposal in any way seriously.

The vast majority of the media in Britain maintain a generally watchful vigilance which seeks to expose, attack, vilify or rubbish anyone who has the temerity to suggest even the slightest liberalisation of the law on any drug. Marijuana remains the only drug where some parts of the press, at least, agree things have to change. But the *Independent on Sunday*'s campaign to have it decriminalised went nowhere, as might be expected. Although the argument over the medical use of cannabis to alleviate pain in some conditions seems to have been won, researchers almost immediately responded by announcing they had found ways of taking the 'high' out of the drug.

On the streets, the situation in Britain is mixed. There is a growing heroin problem and a crack one, too, but nothing like as bad as predicted. Nearly 40 per cent of youngsters aged 15 and 16 have tried cannabis (marijuana), according to surveys, while 10 per cent of adults have tried it. This is the highest proportion in Europe. In Britain the use of marijuana has doubled since 1990 and the use of other drugs is rising fast (from a survey by the European Union drugs agency and Exeter University). Other research indicates up to one-third of all adults aged 16–59 in England and Wales have used recreational drugs (or solvents) at some time in their lives; this rises to half for 16–24-year-olds. In Northern Ireland 40 per cent of 16–29-year-olds may have tried drugs. Possibly as many as a third of 15-year-olds in England and 40 per cent in Scotland are using drugs of one kind or another. There may, out of all drug-takers, of all groups and ages, be as many as 266,000 'problem' users.

The Exeter survey found that amphetamines were in general used by between 1 and 4 per cent of adults in the EU, but by 10 per cent in Britain. Ecstasy use across Europe is stabilising but it is still very popular in Britain, although the most recent studies suggest its use is in decline (possibly being replaced by cocaine). Cocaine use is less common, largely because of its high cost, but use is rising and spreading. Nearly 2 per cent of all EU teenagers have tried it at least once. The research suggested that cocaine use tended to be experimental or infrequent; it was almost invariably still snorted, not smoked.

These results appear to fall within the broad range with which anyone involved in drugs – officially against or actually taking – would concur. It means a sizeable number of people, mostly under 35, use drugs regularly. It means the same number risk a criminal record, possibly even prison, for so doing. It means there are now two established cultures in Britain: drug-takers and non-drug-takers. It means that a lot of people have to be careful in all kinds of social situations; that their natural inclination to, for example, take a line of cocaine *because it might reduce their desire for alcohol*, has to be tempered with the knowledge that they might end the night in a police cell with much worse to come.

The standard line, no pun intended, on drug-taking is that it harms the young and that as most drugs are taken by the young, we have a moral duty, as adults, to protect them against the inclination to excess and self-destruction. The same standard line also points to research (we all have our favourites, here) which shows that once started on, say marijuana, a drugs 'career' will follow, at the end of which lies heroin and probably death in the gutter. Behind this view lurks the ever-present figure of the drug 'pusher', always at the elbow of the innocent, ready with a smile and a shove to promote more drug-taking, and for more interesting – that is, more addictive – drugs to take. I want to return to this dealing side in a moment. The most prominent model on British television of this type in 2001 was the BBC television *EastEnders* soap opera character Nick Cotton, who, while actively pushing (through free samples) drugs, became passionately opposed to them when he thought his own son might become a user.

There are many questions raised here, not least that of the concept of a drugs career. There is no doubt that a percentage of those who start to use drugs will go on through the entire range; some will become chronic abusers, although not necessarily of heroin. Price plays a large part, as does availability, as does social setting. That is to say, and there are absolutely no surprises here, the more disadvantaged are at greater risk from drug abuse than are the advantaged, with a few inevitable exceptions among professionals and the rich. All these latter cases will be heavily covered by the media if they come to light. The nastier drugs are easier to get in the more deprived areas, just as the chances of them being badly administered or mixed with various potentially lethal combinations of other, contaminated substances are higher, too. With poor housing, high unemployment, bad health and low educational provision or prospects go bad drugs.

The great missing middle to the entire drugs debate, as discussed on a radio or television set near you or in your daily newspaper, is this: they provide, for want of a better word, a high. Different drugs provide a different kind, just as wine gives a different flavour, if you like, to rum, or whisky, or beer. That is why people take them: the experience is positive, give or take a few bad trips on LSD, or over-indulgence in anything. At the same time, in the most deprived areas, selling drugs is the only way to make a lot of money very quickly. Folk with few or no prospects find this combination – a ready market of sadness and cash in hand – irresistible. Drug-dealing is born from the obvious combination of factors such as these, not from some international conspiracy.

For the middle-class recreational user little of this applies: his or her dealer is almost certainly a fellow professional; where they get the drugs from is not a question to be asked. Behind all recreational, illegal drugs is a huge and flourishing set of criminal organisations with enormous resources. Some extremely unpleasant people are involved. They are able to move their product around the world, often in very large quantities, because they have the power to bribe almost anyone; when push comes to shove many succumb, because the sums we are talking about here are colossal. If bribery does not work, there is sufficient slack in the enforcement system to ensure the bulk of the product gets through. If that fails they may resort to levels of violence that trained military personnel will baulk at. As a result of this, as well as of a sophisticated system of production, price stability in the drugs business is a wonder to behold: governments, fighting inflation, should take note.

Drugs *are* addictive: even cocaine, after much agonised discussion, is certainly psychologically addictive (see Appendix); it is, specifically, subtly addictive, which means that over time there is a danger of a slow climb in use and, therefore, the threat of chronic dependency. Alcohol is similarly subtly addictive and a combination of cocaine in alcohol, as with Vin Mariani, would – as it did – prove a flavoursome drink. Heroin is famously addictive but not as much so as many public figures would have you believe. Marijuana is probably less addictive, but people certainly become habituated to using it. All drug-taking currently involves a culture of use (witness your local pub on any evening). There have been suggestions that the rituals surrounding drug use – with cocaine, the mirror to chop the drug, the razor blades, the forming into neat lines of the powder – contribute in no small way to creating some of the mystique. Even the illegality of drugs may increase, not decrease, a desire among some – and the young are obvious candidates here – to seek out and try drugs.

Finally, the kids, your children and mine: would you give them drugs? The short answer is that you do: widening the definition only a little. Children get one of the most addictive substances known – sugar, in sweets, in food, in their daily diet. They get caffeine if they drink any form of cola or many other soft drinks. Many are given alcohol from a very early age, at a wedding or a party or, once teenaged, just because it is felt to be OK. We just do not in general want to imagine them being offered marijuana or, God forbid, a line of cocaine or a shot of heroin. But it is specious to suggest that they are immunised from drugs by merely being kept from those society has deemed illegal. Those definitions change: Victorian parents had no moral qualms about feeding laudanum to their children, and laudanum is opium.

In an ideal world no one would take any drugs, but there seems to be a part of the human condition that demands we find a means of altering our consciousness, either reducing the degree to which consciousness intrudes or stopping its normal operation altogether. The very best among us do it by will-power, or contemplation, or yoga, or by a hundred other ways. The lazier or the more stressed, or the more curious, do it using artificial means: we call some of these methods drugs.

There is more, though. Many studies have shown that some drugs, in some contexts, might be good for us – that it is not all just an escape from reality. Alcohol, probably because it is now our only legally recognised drug which does no harm in moderation (nicotine is a complete goner, let's face it), has been shown to help various conditions. Marijuana, possibly because of the imminent demise of tobacco, is creeping back onto the agenda as a substance which – interesting this – can have medical uses. The coca leaf, which is where we began, almost certainly has a range of properties which might prolong active life. Many other natural drugs – magic mushrooms, for instance – have uses in mind-expanding, or just in enabling people to spend an evening having a huge laugh (the best medicine).

We could, if we were brave enough, simply license all these drugs, using the same methods used by the system for pharmaceutical chemicals in use in conventional medicine. It would ensure the quality and content of every drug was known. We could devise a system in which these drugs could be made available in pharmacies on the basis of either a free market, or using some form of individual licence, much like a driving licence. There would be safeguards in how much and to whom drugs like cocaine were made available. There could be checks built in whereby a rising use within a certain period could be dealt with. Using the modern technology of swipe cards, with built-in levels for use of, say, cocaine, it would be easy to monitor individual use.

Just re-reading these words, I find I am shocked by the idea – it seems so radical, so wrong. But that is to be caught in the current mind-set which means that even among many regular recreational drug-users there is a view, often strongly held, that although they 'do drugs', they recognise it is not entirely right. Yet the current regime, of which the moral questions are so tightly integrated into the minds of all of us, is continuing to destroy lives as well as whole communities, here and abroad. It is eating up a huge quantity of money which might be better spent elsewhere. To change our approach so radically would mean a huge effort by government: a huge re-education, short-term derogation from a host of international treaties and a mind-boggling inversion by the mass media, and everyone who has stood up and made money from the narco-complex, national and international. The biggest and most awesome opposition would come not from the United States, but from the international drug-supply and dealing community. They might well be prepared to try to start a full-scale war to hold onto what they have got.

Relax: this idea will not happen in our lifetimes, if ever. Illegal drugs manufacturers all over the world may sleep peacefully in their beds tonight. But if the biggest opposition to this single change may well come from criminals, it makes you wonder whether we might not be doing something profoundly wrong in the way we continue to handle recreational drug-taking, including that perhaps the most intriguing of all of these drugs: cocaine.

APPENDICES

A LESSON IN PHYSIOLOGICAL EFFECTS

COCAINE IS CLASSIFIED IN BRITAIN as one of the Class A drugs (Schedule Two under American law), all of which have an accepted (if limited) medical use, but which are also known or believed to have a high potential for abuse resulting in either physical or psychological addiction.

Cocaine has two distinct pharmacological actions. First, it blocks nerve conductors when locally applied. Second, it is a powerful central nervous system (CNS) stimulant. Depending on how it is administered, specific stimulant effects may differ. The effects are generally of short duration.

The best known systemic effect is CNS stimulation, with the cocaine acting from the cortex down. The cortex stimulation may result in talkativeness, restlessness, excitement and euphoria. Small doses may increase speed of reaction and mental awareness. There may be an increased capacity for physical work, but this is probably due to the user's feeling a sense of being less tired. Early increased motor activity will at first use be coordinated, but as the doses are increased this capacity deteriorates and there may be tremors or convulsive movements. Rate of respiration increases are due to the action of cocaine on the medulla. At first there is no change in breathing, but later shallow and rapid breathing may begin. Blood pressure will rise, and there may be sweating and vomiting.

The stimulative effects are followed by depression, a consequence either of a cocaine-induced convulsion or of a higher concentration of cocaine in the brain. This effect may be produced whilst lower portions of the CNS are still in a state of excitation. With increasing doses the vital medulla centres are eventually depressed, resulting in apnoea (breathlessness) and death from respiratory failure. The level of dosage at which this can happen can vary considerably, making cocaine an unpredictable drug to take. Deaths have been reported from ingestion of as little as a third of a gramme. However, compared with other drugs, cocaine has an extremely low incidence of death; in one North American study it was found that the cocaine-only deaths mostly occurred in habitual cocaine injectors. However, it was also found that snorting the drug can be dangerous; this runs against prevailing street wisdom that snorting, apart from nasal septum deterioration (see below), is safe.

Cocaine has the unique ability to affect sympathetic system functions, specifically the role played by noradrenaline. The sympathetic system is linked to many body responses: activating it increases heart rate, raises cardiac output, elevates blood sugar levels. Noradrenaline's action is similar to that of adrenaline, released by the adrenal gland in response to stress (the body's fight, flight, fright response). Cocaine appears not to directly stimulate the organs affected by adrenaline, but the route it takes in the body and the resulting effects, in a complex chemical reaction, would appear to explain both vasoconstriction (see below) and mydriasis (excessive dilation of the pupil of the eye). It also disrupts the metabolism and distribution of neurotransmitters like adrenalin, dopamine and seratonin, chemicals which allow communication between parts of the brain. Part of the high from cocaine is due to excessive dopamine getting to the 'wrong' parts of the brain.

On the cardiovascular system, cocaine has a further complex effect. Heart rate increases are dose related; small doses will slow the heart rate as a result of stimulation of the vagus nerves. Moderate doses increase heart rate due to stimulation of the cardiac accelerator nerve and effects of noradrenaline release. Large doses may cause cardiac arrest, a result of cardiac toxicity. Cocaine raises body temperature by increasing muscle activity, by vasoconstriction and by possibly having a direct action on the body's thermoregulators. Cocaine fever is preceded by a chill, suggestive of the body adjusting its temperatures upward.

On the eye – the original reason that cocaine came to medical prominence – the cornea can be anaesthetised with solutions of a quarter to a half of 1 per cent; anaesthesia may extend to the iris. Dilation of the pupil occurs through the effect of noradrenaline released from the sympathetic fibres responsible for innervating the radial muscles of the iris. But cocaine's early use as an eye anaesthetic was superseded when it was found it could precipitate glaucoma, or could have a deleterious effect on the cornea, causing the latter to become clouded and pitted, even ulcerous.

Cocaine may get into the body in a number of ways but it is absorbed from all sites when administered; some routes and sites result in greater blood-level concentrations than others. Eaten, cocaine is generally ineffective because of poor absorption into the bloodstream; it is largely hydrolised in the gastrointestinal tract. Intramuscular injection will result in low but sustained levels of cocaine in the bloodstream.

Snorting is still the most common route and the cocaine is absorbed through the mucous membranes of the nose and throat in a surprisingly effective way. At the same time vasoconstriction – that is, cocaine acts on the blood vessels in the muscous membranes to reduce their capacity for uptake of the drug – creates a self-limiting effect. Users who snort cocaine too quickly will not produce an increased high, merely shut down the blood vessels more effectively.

Smoking cocaine will provide a much higher level of absorption far more quickly, but injecting it results in the highest blood levels and gives the most pronounced behavioural effects.

Local vasoconstriction caused by cocaine limits the rate at which it is absorbed, but this rate may still exceed the rate of detoxification. It has been estimated that the equivalent of one minimal lethal dose (MLD) of cocaine can be detoxified every hour. The action of cocaine in the body is ended by three means: metabolism by the liver, excretion in urine, and distribution to inactive sites. The principal route for detoxification is through liver action, where the cocaine is hydrolised to benzylecgonine and possibly to ecgonine, both far less potent alkaloids but both found in the coca leaf.

Symptoms of cocaine poisoning are anxiety, depression, restlessness, garrulousness, confusion, dizziness, dry throat, and fainting. Death is almost always very fast with signs of CNS stimulation, respiratory depression, and cardiovascular collapse. Delirium, Cheyne-Stokes respiration, convulsions and unconsciousness are symptomatic of acute poisoning, but fainting is usually the first indication of a serious problem in many. Rarely, there is found a type of acute cocaine poisoning which results in almost immediate death from heart failure; it is thought this is due to an abnormally high rate of absorption. There are no specific antidotes for the lethal action of cocaine although barbiturates may be injected or, more commonly now, diazepam (Valium). One recent alternative has been a specific antagonist of cocaine's sympathomimetic effect, propranolol (Inderal), but this may be only of use in cases of moderate overdose rather than a protection from lethal doses.

A CHEMISTRY LESSON

COCAINE IS EXTRACTED FROM LEAVES found on several of the *Erythroxylon* species. About a hundred plants of this species have been identified but fewer than a dozen have been analysed. Only two of the species are used as a source for cocaine. These are *Erythroxylon coca* and *Erythroxylon novogranatense*. The coca variety, also known as Bolivian or Huanuco coca, has smooth, slightly glossy, nearly elliptical leaves of greenish-brown, from one to three inches long, with a very prominent midrib on the back. The taste is bitter and faintly aromatic and after chewing a numbness on the tongue and lips will be experienced. These leaves contain between 0.5 and 1 per cent of ether-soluble alkaloids; about 70–90 per cent of this alkaloid content is cocaine.

The *novogranatense* variety, also known as Peruvian or Truxillo coca, has pale-green, smooth, matt leaves of from six to twelve inches long and about one-third to a half as broad. The smell is much more 'tea-like' than the coca but the taste and numbing effect is more or less the same. Although the alkaloid content is the same, the proportion of cocaine is much less (about 50–70 per cent of the total). Large quantities of leaf are required to produce any cocaine: one tonne of coca leaf will yield between 7–9 kilogrammes of cocaine.

Cocaine is ester of benzoic acid and an ecgonine nitrogen-containing base. Chemically it is benzoylmethylecgonine with a molecular weight of 303.4. It contains 67.31 per cent carbon, 6.98 per cent hydrogen, 4.62 per cent nitrogen and 21.10 per cent oxygen. Ecgonine is closely related to tropine, the amino alcohol base in atropine, found in deadly nightshade and used as a muscle relaxant. Both cocaine and atropine are tertiary aminoesters of aromatic acids, many of which have both a local anaesthetic and antimuscarine [combating the alkaloids of poisonous mushrooms] effect.

However, while atropine has a mild anaesthetic action, cocaine has almost no antimuscarine properties.

Cocaine is a white, crystalline, slightly volatile powder with a slightly bitter taste. It melts at 195 degree C. One gramme of cocaine hydrochloride will dissolve in 0.4 millilitres of water, 3.2 millilitres of cold alcohol or 2 millilitres of hot alcohol. It is also soluble in glycerol, acetone or chloroform but not in ether or oils. In preparing a cocaine solution, heat should be avoided as it decomposes easily.

The legal method of extraction (compare with the illicit method as outlined in the first chapter 'In the Beginning . . .') is as follows: coca leaves are pulverised to a coarse powder which is then placed in a large tank or vat. Alcohol, introduced by gravity, removes the alkaloids in three separate wash-throughs. This mixture percolates in the bottom and is then piped to a still. The alcohol is distilled off and the residues are then run through cooling coils to a wax tank. Water is added to the residue in this tank and the mixture is heated by steam coils to a temperature of 60 degrees C. The heat is then turned off and cold water run through, a process which will continue for several hours, usually overnight.

In the morning all the waxes will have solidified and formed hard cakes on the coils. The liquid portion left contains the bulk of the alkaloids and this is run through a filter to remove any remaining wax. Sodium carbonate is added to the mix to create an alkaline solution and benzene added; the resulting mixture is pumped to another tank where the benzene solution is agitated with sulphuric acid and water. The alkaloids combine with the acid to form a soluble sulphate, in suspension in the aqueous layer. The benzene is removed and sodium carbonate added to the acidic solution of alkaloids to precipitate them into a solid. This is collected and dissolved in kerosene (in the early extraction processes, petrol was used).

After the alkaloids have dissolved in the kerosene the mixture is chilled, which results in heavy sedimentation on the bottom of the tank. The top layer of this sediment contains a mushy crystallisation of natural cocaine. It is scraped off, given a further washing with kerosene and then re-crystallised out. The result, known as 'gas crystals', will be about 60 per cent cocaine, 40 per cent kerosene. The dark residue left in the tank will be given up to four more kerosene treatments, to ensure that as much as possible of the cocaine left is extracted. The resulting 'crude' is not very soluble in water and will not pass through mucous membranes (like those to be found in the nose).

The 'gas crystals' are therefore dissolved in sulphuric acid with ice added to prevent any cocaine breakdown, as heat is generated in this process. Potassium permanganate is also added to destroy the other alkaloids. When oxidation is complete, sodium carbonate is again added to check the action of the permanganate and to precipitate the cocaine; by now the cocaine is between 70–86 per cent pure. The precipitate is collected, dried, dissolved in toluol and filtered to remove all traces of permanganate. The toluol solution is treated with dry hydrochloride gas which combines with the cocaine to form cocaine hydrochloride. As this is less soluble in toluol it precipitates out. This is collected, centrifuged and dried. The hydrochloride, or muriate, is finally subjected to three crystallisations from methyl alcohol. At this final point the cocaine will emerge 99 per cent pure.

COCAINE STRUCTURE

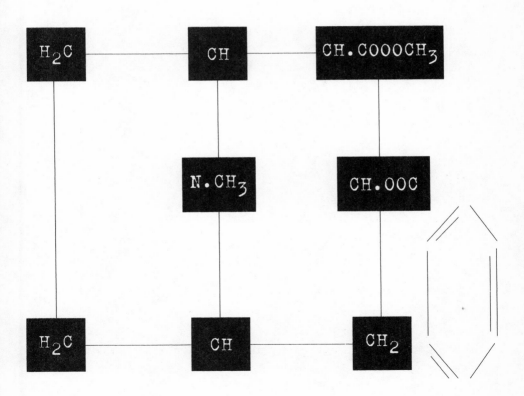

ISSUES OF USE AND ABUSE

THERE ARE TWO CATEGORIES OF EFFECT OF USE, short term and long term. In the short term the psychological effect will be a sense of euphoria lasting from ten minutes to an hour. This euphoria can be increased by smoking or injecting rather than by snorting, where the vasoconstriction of the blood vessels in the nose will lead to a decline in absorption rate as the doses are repeated. Users may well feel their self-confidence has increased; their behaviour may become aggressive. At the same time, users may find their sensory perceptions are enhanced and they may become much more sensitive to stimulation, like noise.

There is a belief that cocaine increases productivity but it is more likely that the effects of the drug are masking tiredness. Sleep is hard, if not impossible, while using cocaine. Users may experience chronic nasal congestion or bloody catarrh. Binges on cocaine will probably end when the supply runs out or users become too exhausted to continue. It is perfectly possible for users to stop, or for use to be restricted by a user to one or two lines at a time, but the circumstances of use will dictate the extent to which the will-power required to stop is present or absent. There is a tendency for many, as with alcohol, to keep increasing usage. Cocaine is very 'more-ish'.

Smoking cocaine will result in a much stronger, much more intense sensation, possibly peaking within a few seconds. This sensation is rapidly followed by an excited feeling and then shakiness. It is followed within ten to fifteen minutes by depression, irritability and anger; some individuals may become suicidal; teeth-grinding (also found in snorting but less common) is a frequent response to cocaine smoking. Smokers of cocaine need repeated doses of the drug, up to only five to ten minutes apart. There are significant chest problems associated with smoking the drug: wheezing, chest pain, spitting of black phlegm and the longer-term possibility that emphysema will develop.

Even with small doses a psychotic reaction may develop where a user becomes increasingly agitated, paranoid, or tremulous. There may be hallucinations: visual, aural or tactile (the feeling that things are crawling across the skin). Cocaine pyschosis is much more frequently associated with smoking or injecting. Users, apart from the very occasional recreational user and those who choose to try it once (and they exist), do learn how much cocaine they can handle but overdoses can still occur, a very few involving death. Again, smoking or injecting is much more likely to lead to this than snorting.

The long-term effects of use over months or years will vary depending on how much cocaine is used and how often, and by which method it is absorbed into the body. The psychological effects of long-term use do include a chronic restlessness and suspiciousness, but part of the latter may well be related to the drug's illicit tag. (Cocaine users face a significant risk of imprisonment for small quantities found on them or at their home.) There may develop over-excitability or over-activeness and a generally more selfish personality. The cost of the drug may cause a serious change in lifestyle if a user begins to increase consumption above a level sustainable by income. There may be less tolerance for stress, more mood swings and an overreaction to frustration brought on by chronic over-tiredness through regular use of cocaine.

Depression may set in, first in the immediate aftermath of use but also through the associated stresses of obtaining supplies, the cost element and a general deterioration in functioning which may lead to friendships being broken and personal and family relationships being put under intolerable strain. Cocaine users will often use alcohol as well and although the combination of the two drugs in proximate use into cocoethylene appears to attenuate the effects of each, in the long term the alcohol may contribute (as a depressant in its own right) to any problem that develops. Some research suggests cocaethylene is a more potent combinatory drug than either used alone.

Long-term users may get chronic nasal congestion and, in extreme cases, a perforated nasal septum (cocaine can burn a hole between the cartilage wall separating the two nasal cavities). This increases the likelihood of infection. Cardiac problems can include increased heart rate, high blood pressure, irregular heartbeat or heart attack. Angina is another common problem, as are strokes.

There is a suggestion that with long-term use the user becomes more sensitised and that an individual's lethal dose level reduces unpredictably. There is a large range of problems associated with pregnancy and cocaine use, and with the resulting child, which is likely to be born with lower than average birth weight, a smaller head and to suffer infantile seizures; these effects can occur while the child is still in the womb and the mother has stopped using within the first trimester.

Sexual dysfunction from long-term cocaine use is not at all uncommon: men are unable to get an erection, women do not have an orgasm.

ADDICTION

THE QUESTION OF WHETHER COCAINE is addictive in any sense has plagued the medical establishment for over a century. It is worth quoting a recent paper on this question ('Cocaine and the Concept of Addiction', by Stanton Peele and Richard DeGrandpre, published in *Addiction Research* 6, 1998). The authors say:

> Addiction is an evocative psychological and medical term whose meaning has changed significantly over time. For most of this century it has been described in terms of an abstinence syndrome (dependence and withdrawal) and associated with heroin use. In the 1980s, however, cocaine replaced heroin as the prototypical drug of abuse. Cocaine had heretofore not been considered to produce 'physical dependence'. Nonetheless, for both cocaine and heroin, current models of addiction – models widely propagated by the media – reduce drug use patterns to the properties of drugs and biological characteristics of the user. In creating this model, scientific and clinical debates along with public debates rely on the supposedly typical, inevitably addicting results of repeated cocaine consumption. Yet naturalistic human drug use and drug taking by animals in the laboratory instead reinforce the picture that use of all drugs depends on the users' environment. Indeed, even the most severe examples of compulsive drug use can be reversed when key elements in the setting are modified.

It is quite clear that individuals using cocaine at very high levels and through routes which increase absorption rates (smoking, injecting) do become heavily psychologically dependent on the drug (von Fleischl-Marxow, Halstead, crack cocaine users). Cocaine does not alter body chemistry in the same ways as, for example, alcohol or heroin/morphine do. Its use does lead to short-term tolerance (the body needs more and more to produce the same effect) but withdrawal of the drug (excepting crack cocaine in the short term) is not generally associated with severe effects.

The psychological addiction cocaine can induce appears to be much more subtle and therefore, in the long run, potentially far more dangerous. Long-term users of cocaine hydrochloride may need to ask themselves whether their use is slowly rising (this rise may well take place over years, rather than months) and in what ways use is changing – if any. For example, occasional use at a party or other event, or occasional weekend use within a defined amount, may not produce addictive behaviour in any form. Users have to ask themselves, at not infrequent intervals, whether there is a slow change going on in which not just levels of use but behaviour, too, might not be changing. If use is declining, there is clearly not a problem. Heavy use may well be followed by a decline or a total abstinence of use as an individual's life changes (and people just grow older, although cocaine is not specifically associated with the young).

Rising use, which includes not just the amount ingested at any one time but the nature of that use (more sessions alone, more use during the day or at certain times in the day, like early morning), combined with a feeling that cocaine is necessary in order to function, suggests the onset of a problem. The cure is almost certainly going to involve therapy of one form or another, but, as with alcohol, abusers first have to admit they have a problem. Discussing this with partners, family or friends is the first step after making a self-assessment. If partner, family or friends believe you to have an addiction to cocaine, they may well approach you, but this is only going to work – unless the addiction is severe – when it is recognised by the abuser.

Cocaine use and abuse is much closer in these respects to that of alcohol – another drug where abusive and addictive behaviour may take years to manifest itself – than to that of heroin or amphetamines. Many people have taken cocaine, and many more have taken it and given it up on grounds of lifestyle, health, finance, social context or lack of supply without difficulty.

SELECT BIBLIOGRAPHY

Anglin, Lise, *Cocaine – Annotated Papers 1880–1984*, Toronto Addiction Research Foundation, 1985

Antonil, *Mama Coca*, Hassle Free Press, 1978

Ashley, R., *Cocaine, History, Use, Effects*, St Martin's Press, 1975

Bhargava, P., *Cocaine and its Demoralising Effects*, 1916

Bock, G. and Whelan, J., *Cocaine: Scientific and Social Dimensions*, Wiley, 1992

Byck, R., *The Cocaine Papers of Sigmund Freud*, Stonehill, 1974

Clausson and Rensselaer, *Andean Cocaine Industry*, St Martin's Press, 1996

de Quincey, Thomas, *Confessions of an English Opium Eater*, Penguin, 1986

Dixon, P.O., *The Truth about Drugs*, Hodder and Stoughton, 1998

Ellinwood and Kilbey (eds), *Cocaine and Other Stimulants*, Plenum, 1977

First International Cocaine Symposium, Bahamas, 1985

Flynne, J., *Cocaine: An In-depth Look*, Carol Publishing Group, 1991

Gold, *Cocaine* (in series *Drugs of Abuse*), Plenum, 1993

Goodman, Jordan, *Consuming Habit: Drugs in History*, Routledge, 1995

Gootenberg, P., *Cocaine: Global Histories*, RKP, 1999

Hemming, J., *Conquest of the Inca*, Abacus, 1972

Herscovitch, A., *Cocaine, the Drug and the Addiction*, Gardner Press, 1996

Howie, James Muir, 'Stimulants and Narcotics', two lectures, 1878

Inciadi, J. (ed.), *Handbook of Drug Control*, Greenwood, 1990

Inciadi, J., *War on Drugs, Heroin, Cocaine*, Mayfield, 1986

Jenkins, P., *Symbolic Panics*, New York University Press, 1999

Jonnes, J., *Hep Cats, Narcs and Pipe Dreams*, John Hopkins University Press, 1999

Karch, S., *A Brief History of Cocaine*, CRC Press, 1998

Kennedy, J., *Coca Exotica: An Illustrated History*, Cornwall Books, 1985

Mariani, Angelo, *Coca and its Therapeutic Application*, Jaros, 1896

Markham, C., *Travels in Peru and India*, John Murray, 1862

Marks, Howard, *Mr Nice*, Vintage, 1998

Martin, R., 'The role of coca etc.', *Economic Botany*, Vol. 24, 1970

Martindale, W., *Coca, Cocaine and Its Salts*, HK Lewis 1894

McKenna T., *Food of the Gods*, Random House, 1998

Morales, E., *Cocaine: White Gold Rush*, University of Arizona Press, 1989

Mortimer, W. Golden, *Peru: History of Coca*, Vail and Co., 1901

Moser, B. and Tayler, D., *Cocaine Eaters*, Longman, 1965

Mott, J., 'Crack and Cocaine Use in England and Wales', Home Office (Research and Planning Unit, Paper HO70), 1992

Oursler, W. and Smith, L., *American Disease: Origins of Narcotic Control*, Oxford University Press, 1987

Parssinen, T., *Secret Passions, Secret Remedies: Narcotic Drugs in British Society*, Manchester University Press, 1983

Pendergrast, M., *For God, Country and Coca-Cola*, Collier, 1993

Petersen and Stillman (eds), *Cocaine*, NIDAS Research Monograph, 1977

Phillips, J. and Wynn, R., *Cocaine*, Discus, 1980

Plant, S., *Writing on Drugs*, Faber, 1999

Porter, R. and Teich, M. (eds), *Drugs and Narcotics in History*, Cambridge University Press, 1995

Sabbag, R., *Snow Blind*, Picador, 1976

Sava, G., *Cocaine for Breakfast*, Hale, 1983

Scott and Marshall, *Cocaine Politics*, University of California Press, 1991

Shapiro, H., *Waiting for the Man*, Helter Skelter, 1999

Thane, G., *Cocaine: A Story For Today*, Newnes, 1921

Turner, C., *Cocaine: An Annotated Bibliography*, University of Mississippi Press, 1988

Weiss, R., *Cocaine*, American Psychiatric Press, 1986